A.L. TAIT

LUNACHARSKY: POET OF THE REVOLUTION (1875-1907)

BIRMINGHAM SLAVONIC MONOGRAPHS

Editorial Board

BIRMINGHAM SLAVONIC MONOGRAPHS NO.15

To Bernice

With all good wishes for a productive

and rewarding 1985.

Arch Tait

Birmingham

31 December 1984

A.L. Tait

LUNACHARSKY: POET OF THE REVOLUTION (1875-1907)

Published by the Department of Russian Language & Literature
University of Birmingham
P.O. Box 363
Birmingham B15 2TT

ⓒ Series: University of Birmingham
ⓒ Contents No. 15: A.L. Tait

ISBN 0 7044 0715 9
ISSN 0141-3805

1984

CONTENTS

INTRODUCTION

'An exceptionally gifted person. I have a soft spot
for him. "A soft spot" - damn me, what a silly thing to say.
I'm really very fond of him, you know. He's a splendid comrade.' Such was Lenin's assessment of Lunacharsky in 1908,
Maksim Gor'kii recalls(1). A close associate of Gor'kii in
1907-10, the brother-in-law of Lenin's rival Aleksandr
Bogdanov, a founder of the Proletarian Culture movement, a
prolific playwright, and, as Commissar of Enlightenment
1917-29, protector of Russia's cultural heritage from revolutionary vandalism, Lunacharsky dramatically participated in
shaping the destiny of the Russian intelligentsia in the first
decades of this century.

Lunacharsky's administrative activity as Commissar has
been elucidated in Sheila Fitzpatrick's outstanding books,
yet, despite the wealth of writing, Western and Soviet, on
many aspects of his thought and administrative activity,
Lunacharsky's singular personality remains elusive (2). As
if in confirmation of his status as a psychological enigma
there are a surprising number of plays and novels about him,
and his principal Soviet biographies to date are a feature
film and a 'fictionalised' biography. In England he is por-
trayed by Robert Bolt in *State of Revolution* as a benign but
politically weak-willed English liberal; and by Jack Gold in

1. 'V.I. Lenin', 1924, in M. Gor'kii, *Polnoe sobranie
sochinenii*, 25 vols, M., 20, 1974, 24.

2. Sheila Fitzpatrick, *The Commissariat of Enlightenment*,
Cambridge, 1970, and *Education and Social Mobility, 1921-34*,
Cambridge, 1979.

Thank You Comrades, a BBC Television 'Play of the Month', in much the same way, but with an added touch of Bolshevik arch-ness (3).

Throughout Bolt's play he appears as narrator and ineffectual protagonist of humane values, missing the point of the political conflicts between Lenin and the other revolutionary leaders. 'He is drawn irresistibly towards the future', Lenin had said of him in 1920. 'That is why there is so much joy and laughter in him. And he is prepared to share them with everyone' (4). Bolt seems to suggest that in the name of that vision, or illusion, he facilitated the loss of much that was precious in the present. The published text of his play concludes with a slightly caricatured Lunacharsky addressing a meeting of Young Communists on an anniversary of Lenin's death some time after Stalin was firmly ensconced in power:

> For life is not secure. The pull of the past is the
> pull of death, the comfort and the darkness of the
> slime from which we crawled in scarcely differentiated
> forms, and the perfect peace of passive matter. You
> see I cannot guess what cosmic irresponsibility may
> lurk beneath my sometime wish for gaslight in the
> library, my mother making music and my father speaking
> French ... We Communists are rightly proud of our
> unique commitment to the Future.

> *He seems about to say something more.*
> *But then thinks better of it. And goes.* (5)

Lunacharsky was a revolutionary enthusiast who exercised a measurable influence on the Russian intelligentsia after the October Revolution, moving it towards reconciliation with a regime which many of its members considered usurpatory. Vladimir Ivanovich Nemirovich-Danchenko testified to this at the time of Lunacharsky's death (6). Seemingly an erudite member of the intelligentsia, he was at the same time personally deeply committed to revolutionary action, appearing occasionally more leninist than Lenin. In January 1918 Aleksandr Blok noted that he was a bit crafty and unserious (*khitrovat i legkomyslen*),

3.   Robert Bolt, *State of Revolution*, London, 1967. First presented, with some adaptation of the text, by the National Theatre Company at the Lyttelton Theatre, London on 18 May 1977. *Thank You Comrades* was first televised on BBC 1 on 19 December 1978.

4.   V.N. Shul'gin, *Pamyatnye vstrechi*, M., 1958, 77.

5.   Bolt, *State of Revolution*, 108.

6.   V.I. Nemirovich-Danchenko, 'Lyudi teatra ne zabudut Lunacharskogo', in N.-D., *Teatral'noe nasledie*, 1, M., 1952, 387-8.

but added, 'He is right about many things and free of many
of the intelligentsia's faults. That is particularly
important' (7).

Kornei Chukovskii recounts how shortly after the October
Revolution an elderly lady novelist of unrepentantly populist
convictions made the mistake of proclaiming across the tea
table to Lunacharsky, 'A Bolshevik you may be, but you are
one of us' (8).

The Symbolist poet, N. Minskii, whose newspaper the
Bolsheviks unceremoniously took over in November 1905, made
a similar error of judgement in proposing, according to
Lunacharsky, something of a counter-coup consisting of an
alliance between the most left wing of the paper's intellectual
contributors and the most cultured of the Bolsheviks 'among
whom he was good enough to include me' (9).

Nikolai Berdyaev reflected in puzzlement that 'he was
a very erudite and a very gifted man, but he remained rather
unserious. At that time nobody would have guessed that one
day Lunacharsky was to be Commissar of Enlightenment in a
cruel and dictatorial government' (10). This enigmatic
duality was early reflected in the fact that Lunacharsky, the
boisterous young social democrat publicist, was also Anatolii
Anyutin, a penner of fantasias and poetry; and in the start-
ling fact that at the time of his death the long-serving
former Commissar of Enlightenment was the author of a number
of plays whose known total rises with every passing year,
and which the latest intelligence from Moscow places at 72 (11).

7. A. Blok, *Sobranie sochinenii*, 7, M.-L., 1963, 322.

8. Kornei Chukovskii, *Sovremenniki*, M., 1967, 405.

9. A.V. Lunacharskii, *Velikii perevorot. (Oktyabr'skaya
revolyutsiya)*, part 1, Petersburg, 1919, 35.

10. Nikolai Berdyaev, *Samopoznanie. Opyt filosofskoi
avtobiografii*, Paris, 1949, 131.

11. Information from Irina Lunacharskaya.

What were the sources of Lunacharsky's enthusiasm and 'unseriousness'? What set him apart from other members of the intelligentsia? By examining his childhood and youth in the Ukraine, from his birth in 1875 until his departure to study in Switzerland in 1895, it is hoped to show how his family circumstances and his upbringing in Kiev contributed to producing the blend of studiousness, political motivation, and histrionic extroversion which are the dominant features of his personality. Although little strictly contemporary evidence is available, interest after the October Revolution in the origins of social democracy resulted in a fair body of informative memoir literature written by his schoolfellows and others which enables us to verify the picture of his youth which he gives in his various autobiographies (12). This literature has been little utilised. The story continues through the years from Lunacharsky's departure from Kiev for Switzerland in 1895 up to his departure from St. Petersburg into emigration in 1907. I have not given a full account of his many activities during this period but have attempted what Lunacharsky might have called a socio-psychological study, approaching the future commissar largely through memoirs and his own fiction (13).

Since the present manuscript was completed a number of works have appeared in Germany which deal with various aspects of Lunacharsky's ideas: Jochen-Ulrich Peters, *Kunst als organisierte Erfahrung*; Munich, 1980; Raimund Sesterhenn, *Das Bogostroitel'stvo bei Gor'kij und Lunačarskij bis 1909*, Munich, 1982; and Krisztina Mänicke-Gyöngyösi, *"Proletarische Wissensschaft" und "Sozialistische Menschheitsreligion" als Modelle proletarischer Kultur*, Berlin, 1982.

---

12. The exposition of Lunacharsky's boyhood in the Ukraine is based on the following autobiographical sources: 'Avtobiografiya Lunacharskogo', *Literaturnoe nasledstvo*, 80, M., 1971, 736-8; 'Iz neopublikovannoi avtobiografii', in Lunacharskii, *Vospominaniya i vpechatleniya*, M., 1968, 54-6; 'Moe partiinoe proshloe', in Lunacharskii, *Velikii perevorot. (Oktyabr'skaya revolyutsiya)*, part 1, Petersburg, 1919, 9-21; 'Avtobiograficheskaya zametka', *Literaturnoe nasledstvo*, 82, M., 1970, 550-2; L-kii, ps., 'Pershi kroki sotsial-demokratichnogo rukhu v Kievi', ed. P.M. Shmorgun, *Ukrains'kii istorichnii zhurnal*, Kiev, No. 4, 1959, 121-32.

CHAPTER 1

THE UKRAINE, 1875-95

Although the one hundred and fiftieth entry for 1875 in
the register of births in St. Nicholas Church, Poltava,
informs us with due solidity that 'On the eleventh (11) of
November was born and on the twenty-third (23) day of the
same month was baptised Anatolii, son of Vasilii Fedorov
Lunacharsky , member of the Poltava Circuit Court and
Collegiate Councillor, and of his lawful wife Aleksandra
Yakovlevna, both Orthodox', this was denied by Aleksandra
Yakovlevna (1). She claimed he was the son of her lover, a
radical lawyer called A.I. Antonov. When Anatolii was four
his mother had a second son by Antonov, who moved away to a
new position as director of the Audit Department in Nizhnii
Novgorod taking Anatolii and Aleksandra Yakovlevna with him.

For Lunacharsky these were very happy years. Antonov
attained the rank of Actual State Councillor, equivalent to
Major-General in the army. The regime in the Antonov house-
hold was easy-going and cultivated, and Lunacharsky describes
his parents as lively and courageous people who would have
made good actors. He attributed to Antonov his first impulse
towards revolutionary attitudes. 'I became a revolutionary
so early that I can't remember a time when I wasn't one. My
childhood passed under the powerful influence of Aleksandr
Ivanovich Antonov who, although he was an Actual State Councillor [...], was a radical and made no attempt to conceal
his left-wing sympathies' (2). One of his earliest memories

1. Copy in Central State Archive of Literature and Art, Moscow
(TsGALI), file 279 schedule 2, item 537.

2. *Velikii perevorot*, 9.

was of sitting curled up in a chair until late at night while
his father read aloud to his mother from the liberal *Russkaya
mysl'* and Mikhailovskii's *Otechestvennye zapiski*. His
father's pointed asides while reading the satires of Saltykov-
Shchedrin made a deep impression on him. By the time he was
seven or eight he proudly called himself a liberal, detested
M.N. Katkov, and pronounced the word 'revolution' reverently
(3).

Lunacharsky could not remember a time when he believed in
God, and would deride religion and the monarchy to his schoolfellows. On one occasion while playing in the workshop of a
nearby silversmith he startled the apprentices at their lunch
by banging the small icon of a saint on the table and challenging
the Almighty to prove his existence by meting out condign punish-
ment forthwith. The silversmith took the 'young gentleman' by
the ear to his mother, but she declined to make the Almighty's
point. She and Antonov were amused by the incident rather than
disapproving (4).

The idyll ended abruptly. Antonov died in Moscow on
2 September 1885 after an operation. The family stayed on there
for a time but Aleksandra Yakovlevna evidently had to call on her
husband for help, and Lunacharsky appears to have begun his
schooling back in his native Poltava (5). His mother, however,
soon took her sons off to Kiev. In one of his autobiographies
Lunacharsky, clearly well aware of the psychological impact
which these events had on him, writes at some length of how
his relationship with his mother now developed: 'My mother
was unbalanced by her loss, and from being a happy, witty, and
joyous person she became increasingly morose, introspective,
and hysterical. Her naturally forceful manner became domineering.
I suffered particularly from her ways because I reminded her of
my father, both physically and by my gentle and affectionate
nature. I was her favourite, and this made her feelings for
me particularly intense and possessive. Her personality went
from bad to worse, but that did not stop me from loving her,
and indeed in some measure being in love with her' (6).

3. Katkov edited the generally conservative *Moskovskie
vedomosti*. He made himself particularly unpopular with the
liberal intelligentsia by his hard line over the beating up
of demonstrating students in Moscow in 1878.

4. *Velikii perevorot*, 10.

5. Sh. Vyadro, 'Dobryi drug Ukrainy', *Raduga*, Kiev, No. 3,
1974, 136; I.A. Lunacharskaya, 'K nauchnoi biografii A.V.
Lunacharskogo', *Russkaya literatura*, L., No. 4, 1979, 118.
The Poltava archives were destroyed during the war (Lunacharskaya, *ibid.*, n. 47) so that this information is apparently
based on inhabitants' recollections.

6. *Vospominaniya i vpechatleniya*, 54.

Lunacharsky remembers his home during his father's life-
time as a place of refinement and easy-going relationships.
With his father's death the atmosphere was poisoned. It became
the house of a lady 'property owner' (*pomeshchitsa*) who
encouraged sneaking, toadying, and every kind of spiteful-
ness. Her absurd behaviour in these years upset him deeply.
He drew in on himself and ceased to trust her. His health
was reasonable, but he was acutely short-sighted and until
he was fifteen his mother for some reason of her own refused
to allow him to wear spectacles. He later recalled what a
joy it was when permission was finally granted and he could
appreciate visual beauty at last (7). A consequence of not
being allowed spectacles, for which he blamed his mother, was
the neglect of his physical education. He was never able to
play any sport, and did not even skate in winter; he later
greatly regretted that this had made him a soft indoor type.
'I was interested in everything - people, books, the country-
side. I had a highly developed imagination and would end-
lessly invent fantasies in which I was the hero'. Deprived
of the radical father he had idolised, repelled by his mother's
philistine values, he looked outside the home for companionship
'I became dependent on my school friends for company ... I
felt tenderly towards many of my friends, and fell in love
with older women from an early age. I began to adore life'
(8).

Kiev had been and was again to become a centre for
radical opposition to the government out of proportion to
its size or industrial importance. The Jewish and Polish
minorities with their linguistic proficiency and contacts
abroad, and the proximity of the frontiers with the Austro-
Hungarian Empire and Poland, made for the penetration of
literature from abroad, while ever-present Ukrainian
nationalism made for at least passive opposition to the
government and the police from a significant proportion of
the city's population. The situation was exacerbated by
Alexander III's russification and anti-sedition policies.
At the same time the social upheavals associated with
industrialisation were further undermining political
stability. In Kiev *guberniya* the sugar beet industry in
particular grew precipitately during the 1890s. In Kiev
itself the number of industrial enterprises (mostly small
workshops) almost doubled from 89 in 1880 to 163 in 1895,
while the population increased from 176,000 in 1891 to a
quarter of a million in 1897 (9).

7. N.A. Lunacharskaya-Rozenel', *Pamyat' serdtsa. Vospominaniya*,
3rd edition, M., 1975, 4-5.

8. *Vospominaniya i vpechatleniya*, 54-5.

9. V. Manilov, 'K istorii vozniknoveniya sotsial-demokraticheskogo dvizheniya v Kieve (80-e - 90-e gody)', in *Put'*
revolyutsii. Sbornik pervyi, Kievskii gubkom K.P.(b)U., 1923,
21.

The public reaction against terrorism, and indeed populism itself, after the assassination of Alexander II in 1881 had led to a virtual standstill of revolutionary activity during the 1880s in Kiev as elsewhere in the Empire. Nevertheless, indignation at the violation of university autonomy by the Minister of Home Affairs, Count Dmitrii Tolstoi, led to a large-scale student protest on Kiev University's fiftieth anniversary in 1884. The University was closed, and in the aftermath of the disturbances M.D. Fokin set up a net-work of study circles among the students, controlled by a secret organizational centre. By science based political education the Fokinites hoped to create the vanguard of a great revolutionary army which would ultimately besiege the bastion of the autocracy. The first step was for members to prepare themselves by quietly developing their own political outlook.

The movement flourished for five or six years, but ironically fell apart through its own dynamics just as the famine of 1891-2 was again sharpening the intelligentsia's latent antagonism towards the government (10). The centre broke up in 1892 still remote from direct revolutionary activity and regarded with some contempt for its outmoded methods, but as we shall see the legacy of its educational work was considerable.

In the changed climate caused by the famine,populists, Tolstoyans, Ukrainian nationalists, Polish socialists and social democrats became much more active and study circles sprouted 'like mushrooms after rain' at the University (11). The Russian Social Democratic group at the University came into being (12). Student circles were soon imitated by secondary school pupils and indeed, according to Lunacharsky, 'developed more exuberantly and broadly' (13). A Polish pupil at the Kiev Second Grammar School, Józef Moszyński, discovered a cache of the students' illegal literature of which his elder brother was the custodian. He read George Kennan's recently published *Siberia and the Exile System*, Alphons Thun's *Geschichte der revolutionären Bewegungen in Russland*, Stepnyak-Kravchinskii's

10. I. Moshinskii [i.e. Józef Moszyński] , *Na putyakh k I-mu s"ezdu R.S.-D.R.P.*, M., 1928, 8-14, 17-18, 23-4.

11. L. Fedorchenko (N. Charov), 'Pervye shagi sotsial-demokratii v Kieve', *Katorga i ssylka*, 27, M., 1926, 23-4.

12. B. Eidel'man, 'K istorii vozniknoveniya RSDRP', *Proletarskaya revolyutsiya*, M., No. 1, 1921, 21.

13. Lunacharskii, *Velikii perevorot*, 11.

Underground Russia, and Szymon Dickstein's *Who Lives on What?*
(14). Without his brother's knowledge he took them to school
where they called into being a secret society consisting of
half a dozen close friends who had abandoned the official
curriculum in favour of self-education. Unwilling to part
with their treasure they copied their materials out several
times by hand and then looked for someone to share them with.
They gathered that a similar circle of protesters had formed
spontaneously in Lunacharsky's Class Six in the First Grammar
School and resolved to sound them out.

Lunacharsky had entered the school in 1887 when he was
eleven. He had not studied well, partly no doubt from his
lack of spectacles but also because of his own contempt for
the official curriculum. Count Dmitrii Tolstoi's reform of
the secondary school curriculum in 1871 when he was Minister
of Education had been designed to strengthen the teaching of
classical studies at the expense of the science subjects which,
like Fokin, he evidently considered to encourage subversive
political views (15). Like Moszyński's friends, Lunacharsky
considered the reformed grammar school and all that it contained
to be thoroughly noxious and an evil attempt on the part of
the Tsarist government to gain control of his mind and fill
it with a harmful content. His teachers considered him capable
but lazy; his marks tended to be no better than '3s', and once
he even had to repeat a year. Against this fairly dismal performance he greatly enjoyed music and language lessons, and
reading the classics of Russian literature on his own. He
read his way through most of the significant works of
Ukrainian literature, and was an enthusiastic admirer of the

14. Kennan, an American reporter, travelled with official
approval through north-east Russia and Siberia studying the
exile system. He published his illustrated denunciations in
Century, NY/London, in 1890-91. The book edition of 1891 was
translated into Russian.
  Thun was professor of economics in Basel, then in Freiburg.
He was critical of the revolutionary movement and particularly
of terrorism, but his extensive *Geschichte der revolutionären
Bewegungen in Russland*, Leipzig, 1883, was considered objective.
The Poles translated the work into Russian, and it circulated
in Kiev in duplicated form.
  S. Stepnyak, *Podpol'naya Rossiya*, London, 1893. S.M.
Stepnyak-Kravchinskii belonged to *Zemlya i volya*. He became
a well-known figure in London, where he founded The Friends
of Russian Freedom.
  S. Dikshtein, *Kto chem zhivet*, Geneva, 1885.

15. The teaching of Latin and Greek was intensified, and the
former technical grammar schools *(real'nye gimnazii)* were down-
graded to tecnical schools *(real'nye uchilishcha)* from which it
was not possible to proceed to a university.

Ukrainian folk theatre, and of Taras Shevchenko. 'You could say the wonderful songs of Little Russia were in the air I breathed' (16).

Moszyński's circle organised a boating trip on the Dnepr, and took Lunacharsky's class late in the evening downstream to the Vydubetskii Monastery where souls were bared. Kiev First Grammar School, they confirmed, could not only sing revolutionary songs but were engaged in much the same kind of self-education as they were themselves. Lunacharsky, currently preaching total abstinence from smoking and drinking and equipped with his pince-nez seemed to them something of a weakling physically, but impressed them nevertheless (17). 'The slightly stooping figure, the eyes short-sighted from constant reading [sic] bore witness to our new confederate's intensive mental activity. Erudite beyond his years, this talented youth had evidently been very well brought up. His outward good manners perplexed our roughish company, but we soon got over the proprieties and became the best of friends' (18). Lunacharsky and his friends David Logvinskii and Dmitrii Netochaev were admitted to the directing centre of the group, while the rest of their schoolfellows formed the first of its many branches (19). Lunacharsky found a circle of youthful radical companionship which answered many of his needs. He remembers, 'close friendships developed, there were instances of romantic love, and I still recall my youth with immense pleasure. To this day many names fill me with a warm feeling, although many of my comrades of those years have gone from life or from political life' (20).

Having studied the history of the revolutionary movement from their illegal literature, the pupils continued their self-education following a list provided by Eugeniusz Tokarski, an elder brother of one of their members, who had been one of Dr. Fokin's closest collaborators. As a result they unwittingly became for a time a late cell in Fokin's 'all-Russia conspiracy', absorbing the tradition of heroic populism, its views on the

16. 'O natsionalizme voobshche i ukrainskom dvizhenii v chastnosti', *Ukrainskaya zhizn'*, M., No. 10, 1912, 19

17. *Vospominaniya i vpechatleniya*, 55.

18. Moshinskii, *Na putyakh*, 55-6, 59.

19. *Ibid.*, 62.

20. *Velikii perevorot*, 12.

role of the critically thinking individual in history, and on the leading role of the intelligentsia in the Russian revolution. They collectively read Petr Lavrov's *Historical Letters*, N.K. Mikhailovskii's articles, and the issues of *Russkoe bogatstvo*. At the same time, meeting sometimes twice a week, they systematically built up a radical view of the history of Russian social thought, reading or reviewing under the direction of their reading list an 'alternative' curriculum of Russian literature, and of the articles of Belinskii, Pisarev, Dobrolyubov, V.A. Zaitsev, and Chernyshevskii from the pages of thirty year old radical journals. Chernyshevskii's *What Is to Be Done?*, obtained with great difficulty, was studied with particular zeal and led them on to his notes on the political economy of John Stuart Mill. Moszyński recalls:

> These unforgettable and invariably noisy gatherings of ours took place in an electric atmosphere of sacrificial exaltation and revolutionary ardour. Every meeting was a joy for the heart and mind, and taking part in them gave us a great moral and intellectual boost. We were all united by tender youthful friendship, a longing for revolutionary deeds and learning.
> The group especially liked to gather at my house, as our attic on Kadet Street was extraordinarily cosy and exceptionally well adapted to preserve secrecy. All my old friends must well remember our furious verbal battles, going on until dawn, in the stuffy attic, thick with tobacco smoke, which nobody wanted to leave a minute before they absolutely had to. The sun was often shining brightly by the time we broke up ... (21)

Stories told by Leonid Fedorchenko, a gentleman of extravagantly nihilistic appearance and soon to be exiled, of the sufferings of the older generation of terrorists fired the young enthusiasts with revolutionary romanticism far from the sober minded 'realism' of Pisarev (or Bazarov). Their Fokinite education concluded with perusal of Spencer (for sociology), Mill (for ethics), and William James (for psychology) (22). Lunacharsky was impressed in particular by Mill's *A System of Logic* (London, 1843) and by Herbert Spencer. These, along with Mill's friend, the Aberdeen

21. Moshinskii, *Na putyakh*, 71-2.

22. *Ibid.*, 64, 72.

logician Alexander Bain, and Charles Darwin, were his
authorities at the time (23).

From the spring of 1893 the circle started on a new
reading list, drawn up this time by one of the first Marxists
in Kiev, Bogdan Kistyakovskii (24). This was supplemented by
a Polish list drawn up in Warsaw. The new course emphasised
the materialist conception of history: the evolution of social
forms, development of capitalism and the revolutionary movement
in the West, the contemporary class struggle. This was followed
by a course of political economy following A.I. Chuprov and
I. Ivanyukov, and finally by Kautsky's *Erfurt Programme* and
study of the first volume of Marx's *Capital* (25). In memoirs
published in 1919 Lunacharsky recalled, with some inaccuracies,

> It was just at this time, when I was in the fourth
> class at school, that I studied *Capital* through and
> through. Although I have since re-read it more than
> once, it was at the age of thirteen, strange as it
> may seem, that I became basically acquainted with
> it, and now when I need to recollect something from
> the great book or quote it - I find that when I take
> the volume into my hands the oilcloth divan comes
> back vividly to me where I would sit in front of the
> light, chewing something and re-reading each chapter
> two or three times, peppering it with a whole system

23. *Literaturnoe nasledstvo*, 82, 550. Alexander Bain (1818-
1903) helped J.S. Mill with revision of the manuscript of
A System of Logic in 1842. He was a professor of Glasgow
University and in 1860 was appointed to the new chair of
Logic and English at Aberdeen University. He was never a
professor of Edinburgh University as *Literaturnoe nasledstvo*
states (664, n. 4), having in mind, perhaps, Alexander Bayne
(d. 1737). Bain's own *Logic* (1870), based on Mill, has as a
distinctive feature the doctrine of the conservation of energy
in connection with causation and the detailed application of
the principles of logic to the various sciences. In this it
may have prepared the way for Lunacharsky's later interest
in these aspects of the teaching of Richard Avenarius (see
below).

24. B.A. Kistyakovskii is evidently the K-s'kii whom Shmorgun
is unable to identify in 'Pershi kroki', 132, n. 13. He was
expelled from Kiev University and went to study at Yur'ov
(now Tartu) University where Polish students converted him to
Marxism. He returned to Kiev in the summer of 1892. See
P.L. Tuchapskii, *Iz perezhitogo. Devyanostye gody*, Odessa,
1923, 29, 49.

25. A.I. Chuprov, *Politicheskaya ekonomiya*, M., 1892, was
compiled by students from lecture notes and edited by Chuprov
himself; I. Ivanyukov, *Padenie krepostnogo prava v Rossii*,
SPb., 1882.

of blue and red pencil marks of my own devising.(26)

In fact, the evidence suggests that Lunacharsky read the book when he was seventeen or eighteen, that is in 1893-4 (27). Nevertheless, he and Nikolai Berdyaev, who joined the circle in late 1893 or thereabouts and with whom Lunacharsky was at this time on close terms, played a major part in developing the circle's outlook through discussion. Berdyaev was particularly knowledgeable on questions of Marxist theory. It is illuminating that the secure intellectual companion- ship which Lunacharsky actively sought, and to which Moszyński responded so positively, upset Berdyaev. Describing a meeting of the circle he writes, 'I was listening to a paper at the private flat of a Pole who was later exiled along with me to Vologda province. It was the first Marxist paper I had heard. It not only repelled me but made me deeply depressed. I experienced this depression more than once in my Marxist period. It was a sense of suffocating, of a lack of air and freedom to breathe' (28).

Lunacharsky is justified in claiming 'I became a social democrat very early on. In fact my revolutionary conscious- ness immediately took a more or less Marxist form' (29). As we have seen, disillusionment with populism was becoming wide- spread among the intelligentsia. The old tactics and concepts seemed to be leading to the same dead end when an influx of Marxist literature, and in particular publications of the Liberation of Labour group in Geneva, offered an entirely new perspective. 'A wave of interest in Marxism completely engulfed all the existing People's Will and radical Ukrainian nationalist tendencies among the youth of Kiev'. The Polish social democrats began to translate Marxist texts from Polish and German into Russian and these were then hectographed for wider circulation by, among others, the central circle (30).

26. *Velikii perevorot*, 10.

27. *Literaturnoe nasledstvo*, 80, 736; *Vospominaniya i vpechatleniya*, 55; Moshinskii, *Na putyakh*, 72,74.

28. Berdyaev, *Samopoznanie*, 125; Moshinskii, *Na putyakh*, 75; Tuchapskii, *Iz perezhitogo*, 60; Fedorchenko, *Pervye shagi*, 26. Moszyński gives the date of Berdyaev's arrival as 'by autumn 1893'. Berdyaev gives 1894. He was a student at the University and was introduced to the circle by David Logvinskii, also by then a student. Moshinskii, *Na putyakh*, 72; Berdyaev *Samopoznanie*, 124.

29. *Velikii perevorot*, 9.

30. Fedorchenko, *Pervye shagi*, 25.

14

Moszyński supplied the 'schoolboys' (they were rapidly becoming students) with Plekhanov's *Our Disagreements*, containing a critique of populism, his *Socialism and the Political Struggle*, *The Russian Worker in the Revolutionary Movement*, and four issues of the *Social Democrat* miscellanies published by Liberation of Labour (31). Leonid Fedorchenko recalls, 'This journal created unprecedented excitement in the self-education circles. Its articles directly answered the question which was tormenting us all at the time - how to apply Marxist theory to concrete Russian reality'. The intelligentsia must combine its struggle for political freedom with the struggle for socialism in alliance with the working class (32).

Notwithstanding his intellectual claustrophobia, Nikolai Berdyaev was delighted by Marxism's 'sweeping and universally applicable historiosophical perspectives. By comparison with Marxism the old Russian socialism struck me as provincial. There is no doubt but that Marxism in the late nineties represented a Europeanisation of the Russian intelligentsia, its introduction to western trends and its entry on to the world arena' (33).

As the schoolboys' circle moved towards Marxism it began to have qualms about its own activity. While the populists might accept the seminal revolutionary role of a self-education circle of grammar school pupils, Marxism seemed to minimise its importance and to demand more energetic efforts to rouse the proletariat. Berdyaev recalls that serious social democrats regarded agitation among the workers as far more important than student demonstrations. This is borne out by Lyadov's *History of the RSDRP* which ironically notes a perverse tendency for study circles to spring up in the 1880s in university towns or places to which the government exiled the politically unreliable, which were rarely towns with significant heavy industry. With little or no industrial proletariat to mobilise, the circles in such towns as Orel, Samara, Kazan', or Kiev tended to ineffectual sectarianism (34). Of the schoolboys' circle Lunacharsky remembers:

> Our organisation, weak and inexperienced, did not yet venture to call itself social democratic, although the majority of its members had become thoroughly familiar with the first volume of Marx's *Capital* and

31. Moshinskii, *Na putyakh*, 74

32. Fedorchenko, *Pervye shagi*, 25; L-kii, 'Pershi kroki', 123.

33. Berdyaev, *Samopoznanie*, 125.

34. M. Lyadov, *Istoriya Rossiiskoi Sotsialdemokraticheskoi Rabochei Partii*, 2 vols, SPb., 1906, 1, 75-6.

the basic principles of Marxism back in their
self-education days. Already we were hostile
to populism, if not to the People's Will. We
had dismissed to the archives of history the
theory of 'critically thinking individuals' who
could direct the ceaselessly turning wheel of
History whither they would. In our minds it was
replaced by the theory that the sole movers of
History were the masses. And analysing this
concept with the aid of the materialist criterion
of History, we came to the concept of class as
the great lever which would bring about the development of socialism. It is hardly surprising that
from then on we began to try with every fibre of
our young being to establish as many contacts as
we could with representatives of the Kiev proletariat.
We yearned to pass on those ideas of socialism so
dear to our hearts which, it seemed, must
immediately win over all those whom life itself
compels to struggle for better conditions.(35)

The circle did not immediately embark on a policy of agitation
and propaganda, therefore, but tried instead to adapt by
setting up more self-education circles, with schoolboy tutors,
among the workers. Moszyński was introduced by friends to an
engraver, Marian Konopko, and later to Anton Karvacki who,
completing his technical schooling, went to work at the central
workshops of the South-West Railway in Kiev. The two workers
supported each other in their educational aspirations and
Konopko later invited Lunacharsky's class-mate, Dmitrii
Netochaev, to join them in what became a small close study
circle. At the evening meeting at the Vydubetskii Monastery
Moszyński's circle had immediately taken to Netochaev. 'Much
more to our taste from his appearance was Lunacharsky's complete opposite, his henchman Dmitrii Netochaev. He glowered
appraisingly from under his eyebrows. Untidily dressed and
shy, he maintained an unbroken silence. With his peasant-
like obstinacy, ill at ease with people he did not know, he
put us in mind of a country boy and we gave him a country
nickname - Mitrei or Uncle Mityai' (36). As a child he had
witnessed a shoot-out in his house between the police and
operators of a People's Will printing press. Now living in
the Solomenka, a workers' quarter near the railway workshops, he, unlike Lunacharsky, had the unaffected manner and
the working class contacts to develop the circle's propaganda
activity.

35. 'Pershi kroki', 124.

36. Moshinskii, *Na putyakh*, 60.

According to Moszyński Netochaev was the best practical propagandist among the workers but, while conceding to him the role of principal organiser, Lunacharsky claims that 'the role of the most eloquent agitator and generally educated propagandist immediately passed to me' (37). Lunacharsky dated his entry into the Party from this period (which he gives as '1892 or perhaps 1893') and this has caused some consternation among his contemporaries. 'I began real political work in the seventh class at school when I was seventeen. It was then I entered a Party ['*partiinaya*'] organisation operating among the skilled workers and proletarians of the railway depot in the Solomenka, a Kiev suburb.' Moszyński, however, says flatly, 'This was not an official Party propaganda circle. It was only the proletarian part of our indivisible circle.' Netochaev did become a member of a small coordinating body dignified ex post facto with the title of Kiev Workers' Committee, which was headed by Yu. D. Mel'nikov for the five months of its existence (from December 1895), but by this time Lunacharsky was no longer in Kiev. B.L. Eidel'man, a member of the Committee, points out in some puzzlement that the Russian Social Democratic Workers' Party did not come into existence until 1898 (38).

Late in 1893 Netochaev arranged a meeting at his mother's house between the intelligentsia of Moszyński's circle and the proletariat of Kiev. Writing around 1902 Lunacharsky placed the meeting in autumn 1894 and remembered it as a culminatory meeting of all the workers' circles with the central circle, at which seventy people were present (39). Moszyński convincingly surmises that it took place on New Year's Eve, 1893 (40). Fedorchenko gives spring 1894 (41). Karvacki recollects here that it was winter, and elsewhere suggests winter 1895 (42). Leonid Fedorchenko recalls the excitement

37. *Ibid.*, 61; Lunacharskii, *Velikii perevorot*, 12.

38. *Ibid*; Moshinskii,*Na putyakh*, 79; A. Sonkin, 'Vospominaniya', in *K dvadtsatipyatiletiyu pervogo s"ezda Partii. (1898-1923)*, M.-P., 1923, 65; V. Perazich, *Yu. D. Mel'nikov*, Khar'kov, 1930, 186-7; B. Eidel'man, 'K istorii vozniknoveniya RSDRP', *Proletarskaya revolyutsiya*, M., No. 1, 1921, 27; B. Eidel'man, 'Neskol'ko zamechanii po povodu vospominanii A.V. Lunacharskogo v knige "Velikii perevorot"', *Proletarskaya revolyutsiya*, No. 2 (14), 1923, 616.

39. 'Pershi kroki', 127.

40. Moshinskii, *Na putyakh*, 80.

41. Fedorchenko, *Pervye shagi*, 26.

42. A. Krovatskii,'Moi vospominaniya', in *K dvadtsatipyati-letiyu pervogo s"ezda Partii. (1898-1923)*, 81-2; A.Ya Karvatskii,in'Iz deyatel'nosti pervykh rabochikh kruzhkov v Kieve', *Put' revolyutsii. Sbornik pervyi*, 98.

with which they embarked on the evening. 'The thought that
we might be the first in Kiev to awaken the class consciousness of our local proletariat was particularly pleasing to
our youthful self-conceit'. There were a dozen workers,
including a carpenter and a shoemaker, and about the same
number of 'intellectuals' (43). There was declamation of
the speech at his trial of the revolutionary worker Petr
Alekseev, and of Vera Zasulich's *Varlin before the Court of
Summary Jurisdiction* (both published by Liberation of Labour)
(44). Anton Karvacki recollects that 'After a social evening
during which there were debates and conversations of a
political character, they explained difficult words to us.
Somebody asked what we should do with the Tsar if we had a
revolution. Some said we should guillotine him, others
wanted him thrown in prison or sent off into exile, others
were wary of giving their opinion. In fact there was a
lively argument. I remember a good joke Anatolii Lunacharsky
made: he turned to us all and invited us to allow him to
choose the weapons for a competition in arguing, and pointed
to his tongue' (45). Fedorchenko remembers that most of the
talking was done by the workers, while, of the 'intellectuals',
Lunacharsky spoke passionately and at length (46). The
meeting was considered a success by both sides, and it was
agreed to set up more study circles for workers.

The circle had by now expanded through the schools of
Kiev until its activity culminated in the spring of 1894
in an illegal mass gathering of the by now twenty-five or
so branches. 'A whole flotilla of boats, which in the
interests of secrecy we had hired at different times from
Prokop, Dobrovol'skii and other boat-owners, set off up the
Dnepr to the estuary of the Desna and there, at the Chortorii,
we held an all-day gathering attended by more than two hundred
people'. Lunacharsky, Anosov, Vainshtein, and Moszyński made
speeches, and revolutionary songs were sung (47). Natal'ya
Satz recalls that her elder brother, two or three classes
below Lunacharsky, was urged to come and hear him. 'And the
seventeen year old Tolya Lunacharsky, climbing up on to a
spreading weeping willow, delivered a rousing speech full of

43. Fedorchenko, *Pervye shagi*, 26.

44. 'Pershi kroki', 127. L.E. Varlin was a French labour
organiser killed when the Commune was suppressed.

45. Krovatskii 'Moi vospominaniya', 81-2.

46. Fedorchenko, *Pervye shagi*, 27.

47. Moshinskii, *Na putyakh*, 76-7.

18

youthful fire and temperament and profound thought. His
impassioned speech was peppered with the names of sociologists
and philosophers, winning quotations and his own youthful,
probing insights'(48).

The participants' revolutionary enthusiasm led a fortnight
later to a protest demonstration over the suicide of a pupil of
the vocational school. The victim, a boy called Knoring, was
one of eighteen pupils out of twenty-eight required by the
school's director to repeat their final year at school. The
eighteen-year-old threw himself under a train in a fit of
depression. The circle immediately invited all the pupils in
Kiev and their parents to attend his funeral on 17 May. Despite
the fact that the examinations were in progress, there was a
large turn-out. Knoring's coffin was covered in red flowers
and wreaths to 'our innocent schoolmate, cut down before his
time', and was followed by a crowd which Moszyński put at
three thousand. The unfortunate director of the school was
asked by a student to leave the funeral service as 'the presence
of an executioner at his victim's funeral is, to say the least,
improper'. Lunacharsky was an organiser of the demonstration
and gave one of the speeches at the graveside (49).

Two of the speakers were arrested. After the resulting
enquiry the two student leaders of the circle were expelled from
the University and exiled from Kiev, while the schoolboy leaders
had a '4' ('unsatisfactory') for conduct recorded on their school
leaving certificates which virtually closed the door to study
at a Russian university. From 1887 secondary schools were
formally required to furnish universities with 'full and detailed
reports on the outlook and attitudes of young persons desiring
admission to them, on their inclinations, material position, and
the social background of their parents' (50). Adam Rabczewski,
who also spoke at the graveside and received a '4', did successfully apply for admission to Kiev University. Four of the five
ring-leaders subsequently went to Switzerland and made contact
with the Liberation of Labour Group. Lunacharsky was thus
punished, apparently in this connection, and his political
unreliability was duly noted by the Police Department for the
first time (51). After the funeral demonstration political

48. N.A. Lunacharskaya-Rozenel' [née Satz] , *Pamyat' serdtsa*,
5. Lunacharsky would have been eighteen at the time. N.
Lunacharskaya-Rozenel' was Lunacharsky's second wife.

49. Bór. [i.e. J. Moszyński] , report in *Przedświt*, London,
No. 7, 1894, 28; Moshinskii, *Na putyakh*, 77.

50. *Entsiklopedicheskii slovar' T-va Granata*, s.v, Delyanov,
I.D.

51. I.P. Kokhno, *Cherty portreta*, Minsk, 1972, 7.

organisation of the schools was effectively taken over by the
students, while those members of the circle who were still at
school concentrated their efforts on building up self-education circles among the workers (52).

Early in 1894 the intelligentsia's drift from populism
to social democracy was dramatised at the national level by
N.K. Mikhailovskii's attacks on Marxists from the pages of
Russkoe bogatstvo. The Marxists had just begun to think
seriously about publishing their views more widely, and
Lunacharsky recalls that Petr Struve's book *Critical Notes on
the Question of Russia's Economic Development*, legally published in an edition of 1,200 copies in September 1894 and
intended as a rejoinder to Mikhailovskii, was sold out almost
immediately in Kiev. The circle accepted its propositions
fairly uncritically (53).

Encouraged by the legal publication of Struve's book,
A.N. Potresov persuaded Plekhanov to publish his own rejoinder
legally in St. Petersburg, using a pseudonym and an obscure
title to deceive the censor. This appeared in December 1894
(54). Again Lunacharsky recalls 'the tremendous excitement
with which I read his book, signed with a pseudonym, Bel'tov,
which everybody immediately saw through. It was brilliant
in the liveliness and clarity of its ideas, and no less brilliant
in form. We read it aloud like a novel, and I can remember
reading it some four times over to various circles of pupils,
students, and workers in Kiev'(55). In answer to the question
'What Is to Be Done?' Plekhanov advised them to 'hasten the
development of capitalism by awakening the workers' class
consciousness' (56).

52. L-kii, 'Pershi kroki', 126.

53. P.B. Struve, *Kriticheskie zametki k voprosu ob ekonomi-
cheskom razvitii Rossii*, SPb., 1894. See Richard Kindersley,
The First Russian Revisionists, Oxford, 1962, 46; Lunacharskii,
Velikii perevorot, 13.

54. N. Bel'tov, *K voprosu o razvitii monisticheskogo vzglyada
na istoriyu*, SPb., 1895; D. Ryazanov in G.V. Plekhanov,
Sochineniya, 20 vols., M.-L., 1923-7, 7, 8-9.

55. A.V. Lunacharskii, 'Pamyati Georgiya Valentinovicha
Plekhanova', *Plamya*, Petrograd, No. 7, 16 June 1918, 2.

56. L-kii, 'Pershi kroki', 130.

Moszyński organised evenings at which these books were
discussed, as were the public debates between populists and
Marxists in the Free Economic Society in St. Petersburg and
the defence of M.I. Tugan-Baranovskii's Marxist dissertation
in Moscow (57). The Kiev debates acquired an edge of their
own. An energetic populist, I.A. D'yakov, arrived in Kiev
after a period of exile and set about restoring the fortunes
of his group. He and his followers attended the later social
democratic debates in an attempt to turn the tide. The social
democrats' champion was Nikolai Nikolaevich Novikov, a former
People's Will man who had returned from emigration in the
spring of 1894. He exercised a fatherly influence on Lunacharsky.
A witty, sarcastic speaker, he was a trained philosopher who had
obtained his doctorate from Bern University. The empirio-
criticist philosopher Richard Avenarius had invited him to
remain and work with him in Switzerland but Novikov, by now
in close contact with Plekhanov and the Liberation of Labour
group, chose to return to Russia. Re-exiled barely a year after
his return for four years to Vologda, Novikov's spirit
was eventually broken and he died prematurely in obscurity.

At one of the most celebrated debates, in autumn 1894,
a social democrat from St. Petersburg, P.M. Kashinskii, gave
a paper on 'The Future of Capitalism in Russia' at the flat
of the radical Lindfors family. This was the first appearance
of D'yakov and his confederate V.A. Voznesenskii, and they
were opposed by Novikov and Lunacharsky. According to
Moszyński, Lunacharsky already had a reputation as a dangerous
enemy of the populist fraternity, and no doubt the debating
technique acquired from his years in the study circles now
stood him in good stead. Moszyński describes him as a
philosophically sophisticated Marxist, but perhaps at this
stage he is better classified less narrowly as a positivist.
Lunacharsky himself admits that his interest was less in the
political-economic or sociological aspects of Marxism than in
its philosophical aspect. Indeed, at this time he was
attempting to emulsify (his term) Marx with Spencer because,
as he explains with a spectacular metaphor, 'I felt it was
essential to put a serious positivist philosophical foundation
under Marx's building' (58). At all events he acquitted himself well in the debate, where the Marxists, before the
appearance of Plekhanov's book, would have had to answer the
populist charge that they welcomed the sufferings brought by
the development of capitalism as fuel for the class struggle (59).

57. Moshinskii, *Na putyakh*, 137. M.I. Tugan-Baranovskii,
Promyshlennye krizisy v sovremennoi Anglii, SPb., 1894;
Lunacharskii, *Velikii perevorot*, 13.

58. Lunacharskii, *Velikii perevorot*, 13.

59. Tuchapskii, *Iz perezhitogo*, 54; L-kii, 'Pershi kroki',
130.

Meanwhile, following on from the meeting between the intelligentsia and the workers at Netochaev's house, and the decision after Knoring's funeral to concentrate on proletarian study circles, new circles were set up among the Jewish tailoring workers in the commercial centre of Kiev, the Podol', and in the Donat iron foundry. Lunacharsky and Berdyaev were active in these. Lunacharsky recollects that the level of some of the workers was very low: 'We had to start from square one with them. We even had to teach some of them to read' (60). Although these intensive study circles were popular they were paradoxically self-defeating in that the more successful they were in educating the workers the more the workers came to resemble intellectuals. Remembering Plekhanov's strictures against the populists in *The Russian Worker in the Revolutionary Movement*, the schoolboys feared that study circles themselves might be essentially an inheritance from populism, where Marxism really called for propaganda and agitation (61). Karvacki mentions the awkwardness of one tutor who abruptly terminated his instruction, urging that 'it was not important to raise one or a few workers' knowledge by a yard but to raise the whole mass of the workers by an inch' (62).

Their sense of inadequacy was deepened when a strike over pay and working hours broke out at the railway depot in late October 1894. The workers in their study group did not play any central role, and they had no idea how to exploit the situation. Eventually they produced a rather arid and theoretical sheet, 'A letter to the Strikers', in a hundred copies and the pupils delivered these to the strikers. This heartened the men who imagined that 'the students' would shortly come to their aid, but the strike came to an end without achieving its aims.

The strike caused great excitement, and a debate ensued in Kiev between the 'Struvists', headed by Bogdan Kistyakovskii, and the 'Plekhanovites' on whether the next step should be more widespread agitation. Lunacharsky with the benefit of hindsight saw the discussion as a precursor of the debate on Economism: would the workers develop political consciousness through the economic struggle, or should it be injected by revolutionary intellectuals? 'We, the Plekhanovites, insisted that the struggle through industrial action was only the class struggle in potential and that for it to be realised we must influence the workers so as to stress constantly the implacable nature of their situation as a class, and show them

60. Fedorchenko, *Pervye shagi*, 27; L-kii, 'Pershi kroki', 126.

61. Fedorchenko, *Pervye shagi*, 22, 28; L-kii, 'Pershi kroki', 127-8.

62. Krovatskii, 'Moi vospominaniya', 83.

that the way out of their present struggle lay in the seizure
of political power by the proletariat in order to effect a
social revolution. We tried to convince the Struvists that
following their formulae we were in danger of undermining the
workers' struggle by confining it within the bounds of the
existing economic order' (63). The circle began to make plans
to acquire a proper printing press in order to bring out a
newsletter with comment on current events. Workers in the
circles were set to collecting material so that the editors
could interpret it in the light of social democratic theory
(64). Lunacharsky claims to have contributed his first
articles 'to a hectographed social democratic newspaper' at
this time (65). B.L. Eidel'man doubts that it ever got
beyond drafting, and comments that there appears to be no
archival record of it (66).

In 1895 Lunacharsky left school. This was a year
after most of his friends because he had had to repeat a
class. Much of his education had been extra-curricular,
either from his own reading at home or from work done in
the self-education circles, and his school leaving certificate
was far from brilliant. Moreover it carried the '4' for
unsatisfactory conduct. His friend, Anatolii Verzhbitskii,
who had also been involved in organising the Knoring demonstration, had likewise a '4'. Verzhbitskii, described as 'a
rapturous youth', and Lunacharsky were inseparable friends
and had sworn a Hannibal's oath in imitation of Herzen and
Ogarev to serve the revolution and the working class. The
Lindfors provided them with letters of introduction to the
émigré social democratic leader, Pavel Aksel'rod and they
resolved to go to Zurich to study Marxism under his guidance
(67).

For Lunacharsky this plan had the further attraction
that it was at Zurich University that Dr. Novikov's mentor,
the empirio-criticist Richard Avenarius, taught philosophy.
Novikov fostered Lunacharsky's interest in positivism and
talked to him about Avenarius, guiding his reading of a

63. L-kii, 'Pershi kroki', 129.

64. *Ibid.*, 128-9.

65. Lunacharskii, *Velikii perevorot*, 12.

66. Eidel'man, B., 'Neskol'ko zamechanii po povodu vospominanii
A.V. Lunacharskogo v knige *Velikii perevorot*', *Proletarskaya
revolyutsiya*, 2 (14), 1923, 616.

67. *Vospominaniya i vpechatleniya*, 55, 337 n. 2; *Velikii perevorot*,
14; Moshinskii, *Na putyakh*, 78; *Deyateli revolyutsionnogo
dvizheniya v Rossii*, ed. V. Vilenskii-Sibiryakov et al., M.,
1927-34, 2, s.v. A.F. Verzhbitskii.

recently published Russian account of Avenarius' philosophy
(68). Lunacharsky's mother was naturally very unwilling to
let him go abroad, but he exaggerated the difficulty of obtaining a Russian university place with his political record
and after a good deal of wrangling persuaded her to let him
go for eight months (69).

The drive of his inbred radicalism, his assiduous extra-
curricular study, a natural flair for rhetoric and popularisa-
tion, for the quick-fire interpretation of ideas and literature,
had set him on the revolutionary path which Kiev offered.

68. V.V. Lesevich, *Chto takoe nauchnaya filosofiya?*, SPb.,
1891.

69. *Velikii perevorot*, 13-14; *Vospominaniya i vpechatleniya*,
56.

CHAPTER 2

SWITZERLAND AND FRANCE, 1895-98

Lunacharsky's earliest works, a play, an epic, six
lyric poems, and three short stories, confirm a preoccupa-
tion with religion, social reform and married ladies to
which he confesses in several autobiographical sketches, and
which he devoted a great deal of time to reconciling in various
ways (1). Lunacharsky claims to have written *Temptation*, his
'dramatic fairy-tale in free verse', in 1896 when he was twenty
(2). Manuel, a (twenty-year old?) Dominican monk in the
mediaeval priory at Ravenna is already winning renown as an
inspired preacher. The following day he is to address a great
congregation including dukes, counts, and even the king himself. But, he tells his Father Superior, mixed up among
strictly monastic thoughts he is constantly finding unexpected
'flowers, dreams, and sighs' (p. 13). He dreams of the young
and virtuous Duchess who gives comfort and support to her
ageing husband. The Duke when he visited the Priory had
said to Manuel, 'Behold the fragile angel who bears me up.
More enduring than all my fortresses, more solid than my
ancestral shield: in her is my strength. [...] See how
exquisite she is, even a monk cannot but see her youthful
charm. And yet, taking pity she loves me, an old man, a semi-
invalid' (p. 14). Manuel with a heavy heart and deeply
ashamed confesses to the Father Superior that he envies their
happiness. It is not that he covets the Duchess, but he
feels that he too would be the stronger with a loving partner
to comfort and support him. He peremptorily dismisses the
rather dim-witted Father Superior's advice to spend the
night scourging himself: 'We must raise our standard, the
banner of Saint Dominic high before the assembly of the

1. *Vospominaniya i vpechatleniya*, 55: *Velikii perevorot*, 9.

2. 'Pis'mo v redaktsiyu', *Izvestiya*, 14 January 1923, 5;
Lunacharskii, *Iskushenie. Dramaticheskaya skazka v vol'nykh
stikhakh*, M., 1922. Page references in the text are to this
edition.

mighty. What sort of time is this for me to scourge myself?
Go, speak no more' (p. 17). Manuel's concern is not solely
with spiritual, but also with secular reform. He will tell
tomorrow's congregation that the time has come for the Lord's
will to be fulfilled. All men are equal before God; the
wealthy must put aside their wealth and join together in a
great brotherhood to wage war not against their fellow-men,
but against darkness and evil.

> Arise, arise! Overturn
> The tables laden with victuals.
> Hard work summons you, creative labour.
> Raise your mighty arms, let your eyes flash.
> Remember who you are. Rally to the banners of
> fraternity! (p. 22)

The poor and oppressed he will also urge to rally, they have
nothing to lose but their chains and a place in the revolutionary firmament to gain.

> To the sound of drums
> [Death] shall lead you to a triumph
> And you shall know
> That you are a man and a hero.
> Look back no more,
> You leave behind no luxuriant gardens.
> What have you lost for your forward march?
> But you shall gain
> Eternal life among the stars of the firmament
> And the name of the Son of God. (p. 24)

Meanwhile, down in the Underworld Manuel's progress is being
monitored with considerable concern. Ahithophel reports to
Satan that Manuel's brotherhood is posing a threat to a whole
range of petty vices in the name of heroism. Satan himself
is thoroughly bored with mankind's never-ending antics, but
his minions are assiduous and eagerly approve Belial's
suggestion that a sprite should be sent to seduce the passionate
young monk, thus diverting his energies from the work of
Redemption. Foletta, daughter of Sylvan, is designated for the
task and the young Lunacharsky gives an accomplished account of
her wiles. First, her ally, the beautiful urchin Uriel, is
sent in to firm Manuel up with secular, indeed plebeian, songs
to which Manuel's generous heart responds warmly. Foletta,
clad only in her flowing hair, follows on a moonbeam when
Manuel is asleep. Violins play, a choir of vernal voices
intones, Foletta advances. Finally, with a change of metre,
she sends in the fragrances of spring. His mind reeling, his
body on fire, Manuel totters on the brink, but as Foletta
reaches out to enfold him he rises to his feet and calls out
to the Saviour of the poor. He will not submit, he will follow
his bitter destiny to the end. In reply, rather surprisingly,
powerful voices remind him in chorus that the children of

Nature find joy and Resurrection in the mystery of procreation.

>Pleasure
>Is blessed!
>In creation
>Is God's purpose
>And His law!
>[...]
>Struggle higher,
>Labour more manfully,
>The dank grave
>Shall have no dominion.
>Burgeoning anew,
>The children come forth
>Through the power of Love.   (p. 63)

Nevertheless, Manuel holds out.

The following morning he wakes to reflect on his bitter
victory. He has saved Manuel the monk, the toiler, the preacher
but has killed Abel his tender brother, the youthful happy lover.
At this point a downcast Foletta returns. She too has reflected
on the struggle and has decided to renounce her elfin immortality
for love of Manuel. They ponder the harshness of a world in which
duty demands that they remain apart.

>Look, world, at the sacrifice we bring.
>Perhaps you are unworthy of it ...
>Perhaps your happiness is too trivial
>That we should sacrifice our love for it ...
>Keep silence, world, awestruck by
>The sacrifice of two strong souls.   (p. 82)

At this moment the Father Superior blunders in and seeing Manuel
with a woman concludes the worst. Manuel erupts and casts off
the fetters of the Order. He is a tsar, not a packhorse, and
demonstrates his new found freedom by making love to Foletta.

>Now I know that I
>Can greet winged freedom,
>That I shall not despise myself
>Nor abate my spiritual powers
>By abandoning myself to love.   (p. 84)

The demons exult. Too soon. United in love and all the stronger
for it Manuel and Foletta resolve the dual calls of duty and joy:
they will go forth together to found a League of the Joyful which
will conquer death. And in an utterance with a prophetic ring,
Lunacharsky's hero proclaims:

>A terrible happiness shall be my staff
>And terrible I shall be towards my enemies;
>A radiant happiness shall be my staff

And I shall be a bright light to my friends! (p.86)

Like Manuel, Lunacharsky cast off the bonds of formal
instruction. He had rejected the Tsarist school curriculum
in favour of radical self-education and arriving in Zurich
he turned his back on the academic courses on offer.

'Just living abroad had a more or less beneficial effect -
the riches of the Zurich library, the extensive resources of
Zurich University, and the high intellectual level of our
Russian student society in Zurich at that time' (3).

Lunacharsky piled up books on philosophy, history, and
sociology and compiled a curriculum of his own which included
lectures in the philosophy and nature departments of the
Natural Sciences Faculty, some lectures in the Faculty of Law
and some from Zurich Polytechnic. His courses were to include
anatomy, physiology and political economy. He had come to put
a positivist foundation under Marxism by studying empirio-
criticism and this, for the months which he actually spent in
Zurich, he proceeded single-mindedly to do. From his medical
courses he retained little, but his studies under Avenarius,
which can have lasted for little more than one semester had,
he wrote,'a profound effect which will last for the whole of
my life' (4). Lunacharsky attended Avenarius's lecture course
on psychology, his seminar on philosophy, and a special seminar
on bio-psychology, which examined his work *A Critique of Pure
Experience* (*Kritik der reinen Erfahrung*). Lunacharsky could
not contribute actively to the seminars as his spoken German
was inadequate, but nevertheless found in Avenarius the
definitive basis of his own philosophical outlook.

'Those aspects of Avenarius's doctrine which provided
the foundation for a biological theory of evaluation were
of particular interest and importance for me. The theory
of elements and characters, the law of conservation in cognition and aesthetics, the theory of sexual affect were all
a revelation to me. Immense perspectives began to open up
before me, I anticipated future syntheses which made me
tremble with excitement. May not all evaluation - the vul-
garly sensual, utilitarian, aesthetic, ethical - have a
common root? Are they not variants of a single biological
evaluation whose basis is the nerve cell's capacity to register positive and negative sensations and discharges and
whose highest manifestation is the dualism of good and evil?
Does not aesthetics reveal the innermost nature of the biological fact of evaluation? And approaching my "faith",

3. *Velikii perevorot*, 14-15.

4. *Velikii perevorot*, 14-15; *Vospominaniya i vpechatleniya*,
56.

scientific socialism, from this viewpoint I already sensed
that it was inextricably linked on the level of evaluation
and the ideal with the entire religious development of mankind, that it was the ripest mature fruit from this tree
which had sprung up from that same root of primal suffering
and pleasure. I formulated all the vital questions which I
would devote my life to answering at that time, that is in
1895-6'. (5)

Shortly after his arrival he sought out Aksel'rod and
was warmly, even enthusiastically, welcomed. Aksel'rod was
not in good health and earned a meagre living by selling
kefir to the Russian colony in Zurich. He was forever attending
to his bottles and had little time left over for writing which,
according to Lunacharsky, he in any case found a great strain.
His style of writing was turgid. In conversation he was
informative but he had a boring voice. Nevertheless, he was
the first major Marxist thinker whom Lunacharsky had met.
They became good friends and he later admitted, half in jest,
that he had had Lunacharsky in mind as a future son-in-law.
At all events, Lunacharsky willingly acknowledged him as his
spiritual father. He took a great interest in Lunacharsky's
philosophical development, setting aside his other work to
talk to him and listen to the broadly Spencerian papers he
was preparing to read to the student circles at the University
and which were to give Manuel's projected sermon its Rotary
Club flavour. Soon after arriving, Lunacharsky attended a
workers' meeting at Aarau near Zurich and wrote a report on
it which Aksel'rod incorporated into an article for the
Liberation of Labour group's newspaper, *Rabotnik* (6).
Aksel'rod strengthened Lunacharsky's commitment to Marxism
and did his best to discourage his cavalier attempts to
supplement or emulsify it with sundry other philosophies.
As far as Herbert Spencer was concerned, Aksel'rod was
successful: he managed to persuade Lunacharsky that Spencer's
view of society as a developing organism was fundamentally
incompatible with the Marxian model. His attacks on Lunacharsky's
other Zurich instructor, Richard Avenarius, were, however,
unavailing, and Lunacharsky continued to insist on the com-
patibility and complementarity of Marx and Avenarius.

Soon after Lunacharsky arrived in Zurich Plekhanov himself came over from Geneva to arbitrate in a dispute between
the Polish social democrats. One of the warring parties was
a graduate student at Zurich University, Rosa Luxemburg.

5. *Literaturnoe nasledstvo*, 82, 550-1.

6. P.B. Aksel'rod, 'Bor'ba zheleznodorozhnykh rabotnikov
Shveitsarii s ikh ekspluatatorami', *Rabotnik*, Geneva, No.
3-4, 1897, 38-41. Lunacharsky's authorship of the report
has gone unnoticed hitherto.

Lunacharsky had witnessed her skirmishes with the political
economist, Professor Wolf, and had developed something of a
crush on her, with her mastery of social science and her com-
bination of cold and brilliant intellect with passionate
revolutionary temperament. He saw her as an almost fairy-
tale figure with her small gnome-like frame and large ex-
pressive head on frail shoulders (7). Lunacharsky was moved
to tears of pride by the oration given at a meeting of the
disputing Polish socialists, to his compatriot, Plekhanov,
although he thought to himself that after Rosa's rhetorical
pyrotechnics Plekhanov's speech seemed rather vapid.
Plekhanov stayed on in Zurich for a few days. At the risk
of seeming importunate, Lunacharsky hung around Aksel'rod's
house, seizing every available opportunity to talk to him.
Plekhanov was perfectly willing to talk. He was evidently
amused by Lunacharsky's readiness to leap into philosophical
disputation with him. 'Sometimes he toyed with me like a
big dog with a puppy throwing me over on to my back with a
sudden stroke of his paw, sometimes he got angry, and sometimes he explained what was what in no uncertain terms'(8).
Lunacharsky found him an inimitable conversationalist, witty,
knowledgeable, and with an immense reserve of mental energy
which he could bring to bear effortlessly on any topic.
Predictably Lunacharsky brought up his plan to complete the
Marxian edifice with an empirio-critical foundation, only to
find that Plekhanov, while he had of course heard of Avenarius,
knew his work only from hearsay (from Novikov perhaps?) and
did not see him as in any sense a co-pioneer of Marx. His
reaction was to suggest that 'If you really must flounder
around in epistemology, let's talk about Kant - at least he
was a man'. It did not occur to Lunacharsky that his fault
might lie simply in his emulsifying propensities, and since
Plekhanov could not refute Avenarius specifically he held on
to his discoveries tenaciously. So far from purifying
Lunacharsky's personal philosophy, Plekhanov contributed
further ingredients by speaking of Hegel, Fichte, Schelling,
and Feuerbach. Lunacharsky had not at that time read any
Hegel, but realised that as an aspiring socialist theoretician
he would ultimately have to do so. But Fichte and Schelling
had seemed to him thinkers who had been superseded and he had
planned to content himself with the knowledge of them he had
gleaned from Kuno Fischer's textbook. He was taken by sur-
prise when Plekhanov praised them fervently as thinkers with
an independently interesting view of the world. The next day
Lunacharsky took his volumes of Schopenhauer back to the City
Library in Zurich and piled his writing desk with Fichte and
Schelling. He was to speak later of the ineradicable impression

7. *Velikii perevorot*, 16.

8. Lunacharskii,'Neskol'ko vstrech s Georgiem Valentinovichem
Plekhanovym', *Pod znamenem Marksizma*, M., No. 5-6, 1922, 88.

which the German Romantic philosophers had left on his outlook and indeed on his personality. Studying them gave him
immense pleasure, and paved the way for his reading of
Feuerbach, whom he was also to incorporate conspicuously in
his later philosophical writings.

> Engels's comments on Feuerbach, to which Plekhanov
> firmly adhered, are in many ways apposite and true,
> but anybody who simply writes him off on the basis
> of these sparse observations without reading Feuer-
> bach's works cannot, in my opinion, appreciate the
> emotional and ethical aspect of scientific socialism.
> Plekhanov, in drawing my attention to the great
> German idealists, did more than he intended. He
> thought merely to make me approach Marx as he him-
> self approached him, but the result was a different
> conception of Marxism which was later developed in
> my work *Religion and Socialism* and drew an angry
> rebuttal from Plekhanov.(9)

As far as *Temptation* is concerned Manuel's League of the
Joyful and its part in the redemption of the world from chaos
and sin exemplifies a philosophy, derived from the German
Romantics, which Lunacharsky was to characterise a few years
later as 'pan-psychic monism'.

> When I was still almost a mere boy the reading of
> Schelling and Fichte induced in me an amazing state
> of spiritual ecstasy, and that radiant metaphysical
> vision has not lost its attraction for me to this day.
> I saw before me omnipotent God who embodied not only
> absolute power, but an infinite lust for life. This
> God is transformed into his antipode - dark, mindless
> matter, a God in embryo as it were, the world-egg
> of the Hindus, out of which worlds gradually emerge,
> crystals and organisms develop, spirit is formed
> and soars ever higher. Fragmented into myriad finite
> beings he experiences thousands of destinies. There
> is no torment which he does not endure, no humiliation
> to which he is not subjected, no crime which he does
> not commit. But in the play of light and darkness,
> light always prevails; in the play of good and evil,
> the good is exalted until at last, at the price of
> all his strivings and sufferings, my God rises to
> his earlier eminence and is enthroned in glory. And
> all of us are revived in Him and are resurrected.
> All of us are now God and remember ourselves, and
> the life of the Deity is enriched by the memory of
> his peregrination from absolute darkness to absolute

9. *Velikii perevorot*, 16-18.

light. Such was the vision with which the great geniuses
of idealism inspired me, and it seemed to me that
scientific monism and the theory of evolution were grist
to my mill.(10)

Early in 1896, after only a few memorable months in Zurich,
Lunacharsky received a telegram from his half-brother Platon
Vasil'evich Lunacharsky who was undergoing medical treatment
in Nice (11). Lunacharsky had not been close to him before,
but the illness became critical when he developed a cerebral
abscess and Lunacharsky abandoned his studies without more ado
and left Zurich without formally withdrawing from the University
(12). He was not to return, perhaps because, on 18 October
1896, Avenarius died.

In Nice he came into closer contact with Platon Vasil'e-
vich's wife Sof'ya Nikolaevna, the prototype evidently for
the Duchess in *Temptation* who comforts and supports her semi-
invalid old husband and whom Manuel admires but does not covet.
'She was strict on herself and on others and often brought me
up short for my extravagant irresponsibility. She was educated
and sensible' (13). Sof'ya Nikolaevna was to become a Bolshevik,
apparently under Lunacharsky's influence, and after the 1917
Revolution became a prominent member of the Central Control
Commission of the Communist Party (14). Circumstances in Nice
were hardly favourable for intellectual activity and the remainder
of the year might have passed profitlessly if Lunacharsky had
not met a renowned Russian sociologist, Maksim Maksimovich
Kovalevskii. Professor Kovalevskii lived in Beaulieu just
along the coast from Nice. He had emigrated from Russia after
being dismissed from his post at Moscow University. Kovalevskii
had met Marx, and his work on the decline of the peasant commune
(*obshchina*) had been praised by Engels (15). Like Aksel'rod,

10. Lunacharskii, *Etyudy kriticheskie i polemicheskie*, M.,
1905, 262.

11. *Literaturnoe nasledstvo*, 80, 743; *Literaturnoe nasledstvo*,
82, 551.

12. Lunacharskaya, 'K nauchnoi biografii A.V. Lunacharskogo',
120-1.

13. *Vospominaniya i vpechatleniya*, 56.

14. Lunacharskaya, 'K nauchnoi biografii', 121-2.

15. N.A. Lunacharskaya-Rozenel', *Pamyat' serdtsa*, 446-7, and
Bol'shaya sovetskaya entsiklopediya, 2nd edition, M., 1949-58,
21, 1953, 503-4.

he took to Lunacharsky and gave him the run of his well-stocked library, advising him on his reading. Lunacharsky argued from his philosophical standpoint with Kovalevskii and with his friends, Professor Yu. S. Gambarov, an authority on civil law, and, significantly, with E.V. Anichkov, a specialist on the Slavonic pagan religion with an interest in the connections between religion and art. Lunacharsky later placed Kovalevskii and Plekhanov on a par as the two most brilliant conversationalists he had met. Platon Vasil'evich, with his wife Sof'ya Nikolaevna and Lunacharsky moved on to Rheims for further treatment. 'In Rheims in semi-isolation I grew up rapidly' (16). Shortly thereafter they moved to Paris.

In October 1896, shortly after his coronation, Nicholas II visited Paris and Lunacharsky, still in contact with Aksel'rod in Zurich, wrote a report on the visit for *Listok 'Rabotnika'*, which the Liberation of Labour Group edited (17). In this article, 'The Tsar in Paris', his first serious journalistic essay, the twenty-year-old Lunacharsky pours scorn on Russian patriotism and liberalism, making up in spiritedness for what he lacks in insight. His confident interpretation of the Tsar's visit is that the bourgeoisie of France and Germany have each, in order to cow their domestic proletarians, played up the aggressive designs of the other and now seek the might of the Tsar to keep the peace between them. In return they will reward the Tsar with investments. He describes the Tsar's procession uncharitably:

> In a carriage, beside a smiling German woman, sits a pale, frightened officer; he is afraid to look to either side as if it is not the friendly populace which howls in his honour, but wild beasts ready to tear him to pieces. He looks in front of himself fixedly, blankly and all the time his hand rises mechanically, pointing to his cap. 'The Tsar appeared deeply moved, almost fatigued', writes one journalist. The French are a polite race and express themselves delicately: they simply thought the Tsar seemed rather silly.(18)

His own political stance is made clear in another passage where he describes the Tsar's apparently unexpected visit to the presidents of the Republican Chamber of Deputies and Senate.

16. *Vospominaniya i vpechatleniya*, 56.

17. G. Antonov, ps., 'Tsar' v Parizhe', *Listok 'Rabotnika'*, Geneva, No. 2, December 1896, 13-16.

18. 'Tsar' v Parizhe', 15.

> For my part I am sure of one thing: this will
> provide the occasion for 'senseless dreams'.
> Our liberals will exult and will begin to whisper
> to one another that Russia is expectant with a
> little constitution. After all it is much easier
> to dream about freedom than to fight for it.(19)

The reference is to Nicholas II's blow to liberal hopes
that he might prove more amenable to a constitution than
Alexander III, when he observed on 17 January 1895 at a
gathering of representatives of the nobility, zemstva and
municipalities:

> I am aware that of late in some zemstvo meetings
> the voices have been heard of people who have
> been affected by senseless dreams of the partici-
> pation of zemstvo representatives in the admini-
> stration of home affairs. Let all take note that
> I shall preserve the principle of autocracy just
> as firmly and unfalteringly as my father of
> blessed memory. (20)

Despite the confusingly leading role ascribed to the wealthy
and the powerful in *Temptation*, Lunacharsky even there goes
out of his way to distance Manuel from any suspicion of
liberalism or constitutionalism. The mischievous sprite
Uriel tells him:

> My brother,
> I hate goodly people ... But fortunately
> You are great in goodness.
> Your goodness is fire. (p. 28)

Lunacharsky reached the age of twenty-one in November 1896.
He returned to Russia to do his military service, but was
turned down as unfit on the grounds of extreme shortsightedness.
He read a couple of papers to his friends in Kiev, spent a
short period in Moscow and St. Petersburg, presumably in connection with obtaining his exemption, and, no doubt mollifying
his mother by citing the necessity of helping Platon, returned
abroad almost immediately.

Like many of his contemporaries, Lunacharsky now developed
an overriding interest in art and religion, although his approach
was, he insisted, that of a Marxist, not of an aesthete. Dis-
pensing by and large with lectures, he studied the history of
religion in various Paris libraries, and particularly at the
well endowed Musée Guimet. No doubt it was at this stage that

19. *Ibid*.

20. Quoted in L. Men'shchikov, *Okhrana i revolyutsiya*, part 1,
M., 1925, 239.

he acquired the more detailed knowledge of demonology evid
in *Temptation*, where Satan, Belial, Mammon, Ahithophel, Mo.
and sundry elemental spirits are delineated.

Apparently in 1897, he took the opportunity of visiting
the populist leader Petr Lavrov who lived in Paris. Lavrov
was in his seventies when Lunacharsky met him. 'He was very
aged and lived in a peculiar burrow which seemed to have been
dug out among his books. He was reading, as always, an enor-
mous amount and struck me as a paragon of erudition.'
Lunacharsky had a number of long talks with him. The topic,
he remembers, was the origination of kindred myths among
widely separated peoples and the laws governing the evolution
of myths. Although Lavrov evidently enjoyed talking to
Lunacharsky he was sceptical of his Marxism and critical of
the dilettantism of his studies. He advised him to enrol in
a proper faculty. Lunacharsky replied that he was 'opposed
to faculties on principle and stood for the completely free
determination by youth of the course of its self-education' (21).

Lunacharsky was far from cutting himself off from the
socialist movement at this time. Aksel'rod was interested in
the Dreyfus affair and its aftermath, including the trial of
Emile Zola. Lunacharsky sent him copies of the newspaper *Aurore*
from Paris (Zola's resounding 'J'accuse', in which he affirmed
the innocence of Dreyfus and condemned his accusers for their
manoeuvring, was published in the issue of 13 January 1898).
Early in 1898 he had a holiday with the Aksel'rod family in
Zurich. On leaving he travelled straight to Geneva, armed with
a letter from Aksel'rod to Plekhanov's wife:

Dear Rozaliya Markovna,

The bearer is a young friend of mine and you
will enjoy talking to him enormously.

Yours

P.A.   (22)

The reason for this, as Aksel'rod explained in a letter sent
the same day to Plekhanov, was to save 'my dear young friend'
(*lyubimyi yunosha*) from the common fate of not being received
for coming at an inconvenient time. 'Please bear in mind that
he is coming to see you only because I assured him that you
wouldn't find him a nuisance but rather the contrary' (23).

21. *Velikii perevorot*, 19.

22. *Perepiska G.V. Plekhanova i P.B. Aksel'roda*, 1, M., 1925,
200.

23. *Ibid.*, 199.

In fact Lunacharsky did arrive at an inconvenient time. He
went straight from the train to Plekhanov's appartment at
6 rue de Candolle only to find the entire family still asleep.
To kill time he went for a stroll and ended up on the square
before the cathedral where with mixed feelings he watched the
girls coming out of the morning service. On the one hand,
well-bred and tranquil as cows, well fed on milk and Swiss
chocolate, they were girls and therefore interesting, on the
other he was outraged by their vegetative bourgeois placidity.
When he returned and Plekhanov in pyjamas and slippers came
down and served him coffee, he expatiated indignantly on the
topic of the bourgeois young ladies of Geneva. Plekhanov ate
his breakfast bun and said nothing. When Lunacharsky met his
daughters he found them typical Swiss misses (24).

Plekhanov found time for several long talks with
Lunacharsky, some in his study, some over a beer in the nearby
Café Landolt. He was working on his Introduction to the
Communist Manifesto. The conversation turned naturally to
the relationship between the economic base and the super-
structure, in particular as relevant to the history of art.
Lunacharsky was most impressed by Plekhanov's aesthetic
sensitivity and discernment and received the insight, again
reflected in *Temptation*, that these were not incompatible
with revolutionary service.

> I remember he was walking round his study making
> some point when he suddenly went over to a book-
> case, took out a large album, put it on the table
> in front of me and opened it. It contained mar-
> vellous engravings of paintings by Boucher,
> thoroughly frivolous and to my way of thinking at
> that time almost pornographic. I unhesitatingly
> pronounced them a typical indication of the
> degeneration of the ruling class before the revolu-
> tion.
>
> 'Yes', said Plekhanov, looking at me with his
> sparkling eyes, 'but see how excellent they are.
> What style! What elegance! How sensual!' (25)

The demonstration of aesthetic judgement was evidently the
most impressive feature of the visit. 'I have never taken
away so much that was truly educational and formative from
any book or visit to a museum as I did from my conversations
at that time with Plekhanov'(25). Lunacharsky wrote to

24. Lunacharskii, 'Opyat' v Zheneve', *Komsomol'skaya pravda*,
13 December 1927, 2-3; reprinted in *Vospominaniya i vpechatleniya*,
95.

25. 'Neskol'ko vstrech s Georgiem Valentinovichem Plekhanovym',
91.

Aksel'rod, 'I consider that my stay in Geneva was successful and fruitful' (26). On 24 February Plekhanov wrote 'Kolobov [Lunacharsky] came to see me with your note. I received him as you recommended, "gently"' (27).

Returning to Paris, Lunacharsky wrote to Plekhanov in May 1898 of the mixed fortunes of the socialists in the parliamentary elections which took place in the aftermath of the Dreyfus affair and the trial of Emile Zola. He found them indicative of the chaos which reigned among the socialists and which had an unfavourable effect on the mood of the workers. He felt the movement lacked organisation. The parliamentary party saw itself insufficiently as a protagonist of <u>class</u> interests.

> There is too much politicking and strife between various factions. Their interpretation of the idea of class struggle (in the sense of the influence of the leaders on the masses and the development of class consciousness among the workers) is too general and at times pathetic. Phrase-mongering is very prevalent. No, they have work, a lot of work yet to do.(28)

No doubt again with Aksel'rod's encouragement he wrote a long report for *Rabotnik* on the election in which he concludes:

> The [Socialist] Party has hitherto been divided into many sects led by empty-headed go-getters who try at all costs to be 'leaders'. It is high time for the proletariat to leave these gentlemen behind to count seats among themselves and to unite for the sake of the common cause.(29)

Lunacharsky's initiation into social democracy continued apace. Aksel'rod sent him a letter appointing him official Paris representative of the Union of Russian Social Democrats Abroad (30). Through the French socialist leader Jules Guesde he met Marx's son-in-law, Paul Lafargue, and his wife, Laura who lived in a modest villa near Paris. His interest in the

26. *Perepiska G.V. Plekhanova i P.B. Aksel'roda*, 1, 200.

27. *Ibid.*, 201.

28. *Filosofsko-literaturnoe nasledie G.V. Plekhanova*, 1, M., 1973, 167.

29. Antonov, ps., 'Poslednie vybory vo Frantsii', *Rabotnik*, No. 5-6, May 1899, 288-9.

30. *Literaturnoe nasledstvo*, 80, 737.

fortunes of the French socialists caused him to make fran-
tic efforts to obtain a ticket to a mass meeting at the
Tivoli at which the principal socialist leaders were speaking.
When all else failed he sent a note to Lafargue who secured
him a seat on the platform. But it was not politics, but
oratory which made the deepest impression. Here Lunacharsky
heard for the first time the oratory of Jean Jaurès.

> Jaurès was particularly splendid. He spoke for as
> long as all the others put together. It was the
> first time I had heard a Jaurès symphony. He loved
> the huge crowd gathered before him and delivered a
> two or three hour speech which dealt with matters
> of principle and all the topical questions, a real
> review of the current situation. The most splendid
> thing about his speech, apart from its powerful and
> adroit political thinking, its splendid rhetorical
> technique and abundance of witticisms and brilliant
> metaphors, was that the audience listened enraptured
> for hour after hour to a complex and occasionally
> detailed political speech.(31)

Afterwards Lafargue invited him to join the speakers for a
glass of red wine.

> You can imagine what a stroke of luck this was for
> me. Sitting among the world famous leaders of French
> socialism. I was naturally overwhelmed and uttered
> not a squeak for half an hour while they drank wine,
> joked, and made fun of each other.(32)

Lunacharsky's other known activity in 1898 was to translate from German Aksel'rod's anti-Economism pamphlet *The
historical situation and mutual relations of liberal and
socialist democracy in Russia* (33). On 10 May he wrote to
Plekhanov asking how he could obtain the literature of the
Union of Russian Social Democrats Abroad while in Russia, and
requested contacts in Berlin, and on 19 May he set off with
his brother Platon, whose health was now much better, and
Sof'ya Nikolaevna via Belgium for Berlin en route for Moscow (34).

31. 'Iz vospominanii o Zhane Zhorese', *Krasnaya niva*, No. 31,
28 July 1929, 12-13; reprinted in *Vospominaniya i vpechatleniya*,
67.

32. *Vospominaniya i vpechatleniya*, 67.

33. P.B. Aksel'rod, *Istoricheskoe polozhenie i vzaimnoe
otnoshenie liberal'noi i sotsialisticheskoi demokratii v
Rossii*, translated by G. Antonov, ps., Geneva, 1898.

34. *Filosofsko-literaturnoe nasledie G.V. Plekhanova*, 1, 167.

Two months previously the First Congress of the Russian
Social Democratic Workers Party had met in Minsk. In Kiev
and Moscow many arrests ensued (35). He carried with him
a letter of introduction from Aksel'rod to Lenin's sister
A.I. Elizarova (36).

35. V.V. Vodovozov, 'V.D. Novitskii. (Iz lichnykh
vospominanii)', in Novitskii, *Iz vospominanii zhandarma*, L.,
1929, 1-3.

36. *Velikii perevorot*, 19.

CHAPTER 3

MOSCOW, KIEV, KALUGA, 1898-1902

The arrests had had a catastrophic effect on the Social
Democratic organisation in Moscow and Platon Vasil'evich,
Elizarova, and M.F. Vladimirskii set about re-establishing the
Moscow Committee of the RSDRP (1). Despite their working in
extreme secrecy they were soon arrested, since the flat in
which they met belonged to Anna Serebryakova, a police
informer (2). Aksel'rod had indeed instructed the young
Lunacharsky to make contact with the Moscow social democrats
through her and he was a frequent visitor to her flat. He
was arrested, in connection with his involvement in agitation
among the workers, on 13 April 1899 (3). Released at the end
of the month, he was re-arrested in Kiev on 24 May and sent
to the Taganka prison in Moscow where he spent six months in
solitary confinement while investigations continued. He
utilized the period to study the history of religions.
Although he suffered from insomnia, partly through lack of
exercise, partly because of the bad food, he nonetheless
regarded it as a culminating point of his life from the point
of view of his intellectual development and the elucidation
of his 'personal religion' as later expounded in *Religion and
Socialism*. He mentions that he wrote many poems, stories and

1. *Ocherki istorii Moskovskoi organizatsii KPSS. 1883-1965*,
M., 1966, 34.

2. M. Vladimirskii, 'Iz istorii sotsial-demokraticheskoi
organizatsii. (Lichnye vospominaniya)', in *Pervyi s"ezd
RSDRP. Mart 1898 goda. Dokumenty i materialy*, M., 1958,
164-5.

3. N.A. Trifonov and I.F. Shostak, 'A.V. Lunacharskii i
"Moskovskoe delo" 1899 goda', in *Literaturnoe nasledstvo*,
82, 590-1.

papers at this time, some of which were extant in 1919 and
which may well still be in existence, but inaccessible to the
present author, in the Central Party Archive (4).

Lunacharsky was sent to his legal father's estate near
Poltava, then went on to Kiev to visit his mother. He had
been invited to choose a place of residence in which to await
sentence and chose, quite at random, the town of Kaluga, some
ninety miles south-west of Moscow (5). Visiting Kiev from
Kaluga in April 1901 he was prevailed upon to take part in a
debate in aid of the Political Red Cross at the Kiev Literary
and Artistic Society. The topic was 'Henryk Ibsen as a
Moralist'. Lunacharsky agreed to take part in a 'pre-debate'
to which many young radicals came, attracting the attention of
the authorities. All the participants were arrested, as was the
unfortunate lecturer. The incident was to provide material for
his farce of 1906 'The Slow-Speed Society' (6). In custody for
a month and a half in the Luk'yanov prison in Kiev he declaimed
poems of his own composition and delivered lectures in the
prison garden (7).

He was eventually acquitted of a charge of conspiring to
distribute May Day leaflets among the Kiev workers, the
Procurator noting:

> He has nurtured a socialist outlook from his schooldays
> onwards as is evidenced by an issue of 'The Free Word'
> found in his possession. This is a schoolboy magazine
> of this persuasion of a vividly tendentious hue. His
> subsequent education at Zurich University, his probable
> contact with the emigrés there, and his unwavering
> interest in social questions have undoubtedly developed
> and strengthened socialist views in Lunacharsky. These
> brought him back to this country and to his involvement

4. *Velikii perevorot*, 21, probably refers to a major and
evidently highly relevant source containing forty articles
and poems from the period 1896-1911: Lunacharsky's manuscript
book 'Religioznye eskizy (Opyty serdtsa, mysli i pera)' in
the Central Party Archive of the Institute of Marxism-Leninism,
M., file 142, schedule 1, item 260. It is briefly mentioned in
I.P. Yaroshevskii, 'Put' A.V. Lunacharskogo k nauchnomu ateizma
v dorevolyutsionnyi period', *Trudy Tadzhikskogo politekhnicheskogo instituta*, Dushanbe, vyp. 6(1971), 224-5.

5. *Velikii perevorot*, 18.

6. Lunacharsky's notes for the debate are published in
Literaturnoe nasledstvo, 82, 280-1. The incident is described in N. Piyashev, '"Arestovannyi" Ibsen', *Teatr*, No. 2,
1966, 77-8, and in *Literaturnoe nasledstvo*, 82, 596-600.

7. Lunacharskii, 'V kievskoi Luk'yanovskoi tyur'me', 1924,
reprinted in *Vospominaniya i vpechatleniya*, 75-6.

in the Moscow case in connection with which he is
accused of criminal activity under Article 318 of
the Penal Code. There is thus no doubt that for
the purposes of the Russian State Anatolii
Lunacharsky is a person of confirmed political
unreliability, but his criminal activity in this
area does not relate to Kiev.(8)

On his release he returned to Kaluga. Lunacharsky considered that his stay in Kaluga played 'a fairly important role'
in his personal life as well as in his biography as a social
democrat (9). Already in the early 1890s Marxist ideas were
beginning to stir in Kaluga, with illegal literature circulating
and a certain amount of propaganda centering on the Sunday
school which functioned in the premises of the Municipal Duma.
A radical self-education circle at the local seminary produced
an illegal newsletter under the title *Foreword* (*Vpered*).
Socialist intellectuals and workers exiled to Kaluga in the
latter half of the 1890s strengthened these activities. By
the time Lunacharsky arrived in 1900 an illegal Social
Democratic circle was already in existence. He discovered
what he describes as an embryonic Party committee led by
A.A. Bogdanov-Malinovskii who was for the next decade to be a
close political associate. Bogdanov had studied medicine and
completed a course in Natural Science at Moscow University in
1899. The previous year he had written a popular philosophical work *Basic Elements of a Historical View of Nature* in
response to the demands of the workers' propaganda circles
in which he worked (10). His interests and those of Lunacharsky
were curiously complementary. For Lunacharsky, the
philosophical young *littérateur* strenuously protesting that
his political convictions on the social mission of art were
entirely compatible with his delight in such contemporary
playwrights as Maeterlinck, the enthusiastic left-wing
Marxist Bogdanov was the ideal soul-mate. A systematic
scientist and practical party worker with considerable
experience of illegal work in Russia, but aware also of the
value and practical necessity of a simple revolutionary
ideology, he must have exerted a restraining influence on
Lunacharsky's flights of fancy even as he revealed a means

8. *Literaturnoe nasledstvo*, 82, 598.

9. *Velikii perevorot*, 21.

10. A.A. Bogdanov, *Osnovnye elementy istoricheskogo vzglyada
na prirodu*, SPb., 1899. *Entsiklopedicheskii slovar' tovari-
shchestva Granat*, 7th edition, 41, M., 1925, part 1, appendix,
col. 30.

of reconciling the interests of the member of the intelligentsia with the moral and social obligations of the revolutionary (11).

Besides Bogdanov, the social democrats V.A. Bazarov-Rudnev and I.I. Skvortsov-Stepanov were temporarily in Kaluga. Lunacharsky notes that they all shared an interest in the philosophical aspect of Marxism and in 'reinforcing' its epistemological (gnoseological), ethical and aesthetic aspects, rejecting both what they saw as the rigid rationalistic orthodoxy of Plekhanov and the neo-Kantian heresies of the 'legal Marxists' (12). Lunacharsky's attempts in Kaluga to get into print were, however, unavailing. 'I had to swallow not a few "courteous" rejections from publishers who as far as I could tell had not even bothered to glance through articles signed with a wholly unknown name' (13). The background and interests of Lunacharsky and Bogdanov made them natural opponents of the growing influence of legal Marxism with its emphasis increasingly on abstract philosophical questions remote from practical revolutionary agitation.

One of the reasons Kaluga was used as a place of exile was its relatively modest state of industrialisation. Besides the railway depot, the main enterprises were the Howard factories and the Goncharov Linen Mill. Lunacharsky soon made the acquantance of Dmitrii Dmitrievich Goncharov and his wife, Vera Konstantinovna, who owned the historical Linen Mill (14). Goncharov was a philanthropic employer who had introduced an eight-hour working day and a profit-sharing scheme for his employees. He was soon on good terms with Lunacharsky, who fell platonically in love with his wife, and had no objection to the spread of socialist propaganda among his workers. The Party historian Vladimir Nevskii comments, 'Where but in Russia, with the most patriarchal vestiges of feudalism existing happily side by side with the last word in capitalist technology, could you conduct revolutionary propaganda in the factory of a manufacturer who kept the company of social democrats and who on their recommendation had introduced the eight-hour working day?' (15).

11. An excellent analysis of the similarities and dissimilarities between Lunacharsky's and Bogdanov's views is contained in Kendall E. Bailes, 'Bogdanov, Lunacharsky and the Crisis of Bolshevism, 1908-1909', unpublished essay for the M.A. in the Faculty of Political Science and for the Certificate of the Russian Institute, Columbia University, New York, 1966, 91-107.

12. *Velikii perevorot*, 21-2.

13. *Literaturnoe nasledstvo*, 82, 552.

14. V. [ladimir Ivanovich] Nevskii, *Ocherki po istorii Russkoi Kommunisticheskoi partii*, 2nd edition, 1, L., 1925 [1926], 483-4.

15. *Ibid.*, 485.

Ol'ga Knipper, later the wife of Anton Chekhov, began
her acting career in the Goncharov's amateur theatre in 1894-5.
M. Turovskaya recalls:

> The estate had a marvellous overgrown path with a
> summer-house, an old-world country house with
> fifty-two rooms where the tables were always set
> and dependants, beggars, invited and uninvited
> guests abounded [...] Ol'ga Leonardovna [Knipper]
> was particularly friendly with the eldest son,
> Dmitrii Goncharov, who sported a red calico peasant
> shirt and slept on boards, imitating Rakhmetov,
> the hero of Chernyshevskii's novel, *What Is To Be
> Done?* He was later on friendly terms with
> Lunacharsky. He befriended the workers and clerks
> of the paper mill which belonged to the estate.
> Amateur dramatics were organised with their
> participation and for their benefit. The perform-
> ances became a popular occurrence; to all intents
> and purposes it was an amateur theatre. The
> theatre even had its own permanent stage and
> auditorium. Some of the young people researched
> into the family archives and discovered that one
> of the wings, currently used as a tavern, had
> connections with Pushkin [who had married Natal'ya
> Nikolaevna Goncharova] [...] The young amateur
> actors erected their own stage, painted their
> own flats, and scrubbed the floors. Here they
> rehearsed, here the performances took place ...
> People drove over to the performances from the
> nearby villages and hamlets. The audience included
> a fair cross-section of the working population.(16)

Lunacharsky soon moved into the Linen Mill permanently,
ostensibly to escape from the surveillance of the local con-
stabulary (17). He was in his element in this cultural oasis
and willingly participated in the Goncharovs' many enterprises.
Since a copy of *Temptation* was made by one of the Goncharov
workers he undoubtedly read it there and indeed, given the
similarity of Manuel's mission to convert the rich to the
Dominican cause and Lunacharsky's relationship with Goncharov,
we may surmise that if the play was not in fact written there,
it may well have been revised in these months. The atmosphere inspired him to a prodigious outpouring of poetry,
mostly lyrical but including an exceedingly long epic.

16. M. Turovskaya, *Ol'ga Leonardovna Knipper-Chekhova*, M.,
1959, 15-16.

17. *Velikii perevorot*, 22-3.

The poetry of a gifted amateur, these poems, none of
which has yet been published in its entirety, mostly
testify to Lunacharsky's inclination to the style of the
'Silver Age'. The themes of *Temptation* recur in *March of
the Twentieth Century*, written on 30 December 1900 for singing, apparently, to the tune of the *Internationale*.

Вперед! - чтоб не было
   голодных,
Раздетых, нищих и сирот.
Да сядет в сонме благородных
В труде проливший честно пот.
	Forward! Let there be no
	   more hunger,
	No more naked, no more beggars
	   and orphans.
	Let those who have sweated in
	   honest labour
	Take their place among the
	   assembly of the exalted.

(18)

A visitor to the Linen Mill during the summer of 1901
was the pianist E. Gnesina who recalls boating trips on fine
days when Lunacharsky, standing in the boat, would recite
extensively from Pushkin and Lermontov and from his own poems.
'We never ceased to be amazed at the expressiveness of his
declamation and at his phenomenal memory which seemed to know
no bounds. Anatolii Vasil'evich could recite poetry for hours
on end and, surprisingly enough, we were never tired or bored
by him. Our evenings were devoted to music. The Goncharovs
would sing, and I accompanied them and played Chopin. Anatolii
Vasil'evich was our splendidly attentive audience' (19). And
indeed, in just sixteen days that June, Lunacharsky himself
responded with an epic entitled *Music. A Dithyramb to Dionysos*.
In a strikingly 'modernist' idiom the narrator invokes Dionysos
to inspire his poem:

Бывали времена, когда душа в
   волненьи
Звенела, как нестройная струна,
Сжималась с болию и рвалась в
   исступленьи
И позабыть успев холодные
   ученья
Просила Бога скорбию полна.
	There have been times when
	   my spirit in agitation
	Jangled like an untuned string,
	Contracted in pain and thrashed
	   about in frenzy
	And forgetful of sobre doctrines
	Full of anguish cried out to God.

18. *Marsh XX veka*, quoted in Yaroshevskii, 'Put' A.V.
Lunacharskogo', 224. See also N.A. Trifonov, 'O Lunacharskom -
poete', *Russkaya literatura*, No. 4, 1975, 138.

19. E. Gnesina, 'Vospominaniya o Lunacharskom', *Sovetskaya
muzyka*, No. 3, 1967, 71.

Напрасно разум мой холодною
    рукою
Старался удержат порыв души:
С неудержимою, стихийною
    тоскою
Звала, звала она в ночной тиши.
	In vain my reason with a leaden
	    hand
	Tried to restrain the impulse of
	    my soul
	With uncontrollable, spontaneous
	    yearning
	In the still of the night it
	    cried to you

И ты ей отвечал!	And you replied.

(20)

The poem continues through cantos entitled 'The Bowels of the
Universe', 'Solace', 'To Arms', 'Love', and 'Death' (21).
Science and reason are not enough. Beauty is the ultimate
religion and, at least for the purposes of the poem, anyone
unrestrainedly living life to the full in the realm of the
imagination and of music is advancing the divine purpose and
bringing closer the day 'our world will be reconciled with
beauty'. Lunacharsky's Fichtean-Schellingian synthesis rings
out loud and clear.

Но мир - он вечен! вспомним
    в нем
Мы как одно всегда живем!
В нем смерти нет! в нем
    вечный Бог
Творит роскошный свой чертог.
	But the world endures.
	    Remember as parts of it
	We are eternally alive as
	    one being.
	In that there is no death!
	    So does God Eternal
	Build his magnificent palace.

(22)

The exuberant young revolutionary concludes his epic with a
ringing call for the collective creation of beauty.

20. *Muzyka.* *Difiramb bogu Dionisu*, Gorky Institute of World
Literature (IMLI), M., file 16, schedule 1, item No. 30, 2-3.

21. 'Nedra vselennoi', 'Uteshenie', 'K oruzhiyu', 'Lyubov'',
'Smert''.

22. *Ibid.*, 46.

Опьянимся соком винограда,	Let us intoxicate ourselves
Дифирамб звучнее запоем,	with the juice of the grape
Полетим в забвенье чрез	Let our dithyramb ring out
преграды -	loud and strong
Поцелуй с уст Бахуса сорвем.	Let us in our ecstasy break
Смерть прийди! нас ждет с	down all the barriers
тобой награда:	And steal a kiss from the lips
В нашем сердце все мы оживем.	of Bacchus.
Эвоэ! о дайте, братья, руки,	Be welcome, Death! A just
Позабудь, что ты есть только	reward awaits us
ты,	In our hearts we all shall
Будем Мы! и среди моря муки	live again.
Создалим мгновенье красоты.	Evoe! Give me your hands, my
	brothers
	And forget that you are only
	you -
	Let us be We! and in a sea of
	misery
	Create great beauty for an
	instant too.

(23)

As has been mentioned, Lunacharsky fell in love with Goncharov's
wife, Vera Konstantinovna, in whose gold monogrammed notebook
the fair copy of the Dithyramb to Dionysos is written. Many of
his poems seem mere flirtatious evidence of virtuosity, for
example the earliest - To a Portrait - is inscribed 'Just for
you my angel - a Minnesang in the style of the old troubadours'
(24). After a suitably archaic parody of courtly love poetry,
Lunacharsky concludes with mock menace:

Но, дама-чудная, на	But, wondrous lady, it may be
непослушной лире	That on my disobedient lyre
Быть может зазвучит	Unbridled passion may sound
разнузданная страсть	forth
Как резкий диссонанс прорвется	In harsh disharmony the voice
вдруг мольбою	Of my most wretched longing
Мой горестный порыв к любви	For earthly love, for you
земной, к тебе:	And in your presence near the
И струны зазвенят безумно пред	strings
тобою	Ring out a curse to fate so
Проклятие безжалостной судьбе.	pitiless.

23. Ibid., 46v.

24. K portretu. Minnesang vo vkuse starykh trubadurov, IMLI,
file 16, schedule 1, item No. 29.

That Lunacharsky was intent primarily on display is further
suggested by the legend between this and another poem copied
on to the same sheet on the same day which runs: 'There ...
and here's another'. The next poem is an evocation of the
writhings of an awakening heart as it tries to recall the
cause of its present agitation. Frustration enfolds the poet
and he seems to hear a melancholy far distant song of a choir.

Зовут!... Словно голос любимого друга	Someone's calling. In the song I seem to hear
Доносится с песней и манит и просит,	The voice of a dear friend inviting me, urging me;
Как будто дыхания моря и юга	A breeze from the sea and from southern lands
С собой эти влажные звуки приносит.	Seems to sigh in these sultry sounds
И мучится сердце, и хочет и рвется,	And my aching heart yearns - eager,
И полно слезами, мечтою, порывом	Tremulous, restless, full of hope,
И полно любовью, и бьется, и бьется	And love - pounding, and pounding ...

(25)

Several of the poems are distinctly challenging and
suggest a role for Lunacharsky in the Goncharovs' country
ménage somewhere between the platonic frustration of Turgenev's
Rakitin and the careless youthful potency of Belyaev. On
23 September 1901 he wrote a conceit in which he imagines himself a flower in the garden where his beloved strolls. She
reaches out a hand to take him and he exhales his sweet fragrance
towards her. She breaks his stem but is overcome. At this
point his elder brother (of a flower?) comes by and warns her
of the deadly poison which the flower secretes. The sweeter
the fragrance of this particular flower the more severely all
around will cry 'Keep away from it!' (26).

In moments of depression Lunacharsky's alter ego could
advocate an aesthete's disdain for the world and all its work.
In another poem he likens his soul at such times to a lake in
turmoil during a thunderstorm. A malevolent gnome flies over
the lake on the forks of lightning.

25. *Tak stranno ... Nezrimym ob"yat'em tomlen'e*, IMLI, *ibid.*,
2v.

26. *Mne snilos', chto ya stal tsvetkom*, IMLI, *ibid.*, item No.
27.

"Умри! умри!" шипит он:
"вечно
Продлится тягостная мгла.
Ты видел свет, душа конечно
Снести утраты не смогла.
Умри! отбрось с презрением
  блюдо.
На нем об"едки, посмотри!
Обман, обман: об"едков
  груда:
Отбрось - умри! отбрось
  - умри!

"Die! Die!" he hisses. "This
Depressing gloom will last
  forever
You have known the light, how
  could your soul
Endure such loss?
Die! Cast aside contemptuously
The proffered plate of half-
  chewed scraps.
Illusion, illusion! Disdain
  these left-overs.
Disdain, and die! Disdain,
  and die!"

(27)

However, he did not follow his gnome's advice or his story
would be very different. Lunacharsky's time in the limbo
of Kaluga was coming to an end. In elegiac mood he drank in
the surroundings he would shortly have to leave.

Ах, прошло мое лето и осень
  пришла
Осень горько-печальной разлуки!
И последние дни, доцветают они
Полны сладкотомительной муки!
О последние дни, надо пить вас
  как мед
Старый мед золотистый и
  сладкий,
Каждый миг надо пить с упоенной
  душой,
Каждый миг быстролетный и
  краткий.

My summer is gone and autumn
  is come
An autumn of distressful
  parting.
As the leaves change colour,
  these last few days
Are filled with sweet torment
O, departing days let us
  savour you like honey,
Old honey, golden and sweet.
Let us savour each moment
  enraptured
Each moment fugitive and
  brief.

(28)

The Goncharovs left for Moscow; Lunacharsky's colleagues
were dispersed to their respective places of exile. As his
own case dragged on he threw himself single-mindedly into
lecturing to study circles from the purely literary (for shop
assistants), to the radical (attended nervously by an assistant
of the Governor of Kaluga), to the agitational (among the workers
at the railway depot) (29). On 26 January 1902 Lunacharsky
left the Linen Mill. His case still had not been decided by
the authorities, but he set off with permission to join some
of his friends in Vologda, stopping on the way in Moscow to
visit Ol'ga Knipper and to read *Temptation* to her. Knipper
was an actress of the Moscow Art Theatre, which was then

27. IMLI, *ibid.*, item No. 28, 3.

28. *Zolotoe utro*, IMLI, *ibid.*, item No. 26.

29. *Velikii perevorot*, 24.

rapidly rising to the height of its renown. She wrote that
evening to Chekhov, 'Today a chap called Lunacharsky read me
his play: a - don't be put off - dramatic fairy-tale in verse.
He's a character rather like Sulerzhitskii'(30). Knipper was
evidently fairly impressed with him, although she reserved
judgement, having seen him only twice. *Temptation*, she felt,
might provide an interesting theme for an opera (31).

Chekhov's reply was irritable and perhaps tinged with
jealousy. 'You are in raptures over L.'s play, but this is
the play of a dilettante, written in a solemn classical
style because the author does not know how to write simply,
from Russian life. This L. has, I think, been writing for
a long time and if you were to dig about you would probably
find I have letters from him'. He later wrote that a Dr.
Chlenov who had been present at the playreading had written
to him to say it had 'driven him to desperation' (32).
Perhaps the unkindest cut was Knipper's subsequent denial of
any enthusiasm for the play: 'Antonchik, I am not in the least
enraptured by L.'s play. What gave you that impression?
Was that really how you read my letter?' (33).

30. L.A. Sulerzhitskii (1872-1916). Manual labourer, associate
of L.N. Tolstoi. Exiled for refusing as a conscript to swear
allegiance to the Tsar. He helped to organize the emigration
of the Dukhobors to Canada in 1898. 1900-1902 came into contact
through Gorky and Chekhov with the Moscow Art Theatre. 1912-
1916 Director of the theatre's First Studio.

31. Letter of 26 January 1902 from Knipper to Chekhov in
Perepiska A.P. Chekhova i O.L. Knipper, 2, M., 1934, 282-3.

32. Letter of 31 January 1902, *ibid.*, 293; letter of 2
February 1902, *ibid.*, 298.

33. Letter of 4 February 1902, *ibid.*, 302-3. It is not
clear that Chekhov had actually read *Temptation*. He may
have formed his judgement from Knipper's slightly ironical
description of the plot in her original letter.

CHAPTER 4

VOLOGDA,   TOT'MA, 1902-4

> I travelled to Vologda in the winter of 1902 after
> a period of severe illness.
> I was still convalescing when I arrived in the snow-
> covered town which that day lay sparkling in the sun-
> shine. And just for that reason, as I stepped down
> unsteadily on to the station platform, I received my
> first impression of Vologda in an unusually joyful
> frame of mind. I was coming back to life physically
> and took in my surroundings with especial pleasure.(1)

        On his first day Lunacharsky was reunited with old friends.
Many Social Democrats from the Kiev Committee had been exiled
there in 1900 (2). Other exiles included the writer Aleksei
Remizov, the future leader of the terrorist section of the
Socialist Revolutionary Party, Boris Savinkov, the historian
of the Decembrist movement, P.E. Shchegolev, and Nikolai
Berdyaev, one of the leaders of the Kiev schoolboy conspiratorial
organization who, as Lunacharsky put it, 'had at the time moved
a long way from us, but who was of great interest to us
precisely as an opponent' (3). Berdyaev had just published
his first book, which had a long introduction by the foremost
legal Marxist, Petr Struve, and he was, according to Lunacharsky,
on his way to dominating the intellectual scene in Vologda (4).

1. 'Iz vologodskikh vospominanii', *Sever*, No. 2, Vologda,
1923, 1.

2. I.E. Ermolaev, 'Moi vospominaniya', *Sever*, No. 3-4,
1923, 4.

3. *Velikii perevorot*, 25.

4. N.A. Berdyaev, *Sub"ektivizm i individualizm v obshchestvennoi filosofii*, SPb., 1900.

Public lectures were given before an audience of fifty or
sixty exiles and local inhabitants by Bogdanov, Igor'
Kistyakovskii, A.S. Suvorov, a Marxist who was one of the
first intellectuals to be exiled to Vologda, and Berdyaev.
Apparently the intellectual discussion was often rather above
the heads of the audience (5). Nonetheless, the fact that
Bogdanov and Suvorov were left-wing Marxists while Kistyakovskii
and Berdyaev were legal Marxists allowed passions to run high.
It was precisely in this area that Lunacharsky upon his arrival
operated with great success and the struggle between the two
sides reached its height. Despite repeated invitations Berdyaev
declined to confront Lunacharsky in public (6). He ceased to
lecture, and in April 1902 left Vologda altogether (7).
Lunacharsky seems to have followed the practice he had learned
as a schoolboy of reviewing the latest publications from his
own political standpoint. He subsequently wrote up the lectures
as reviews for such major journals as *Obrazovanie* and *Russkaya
mysl'* (8).

At the same time Lunacharsky set out to attack the ethics
of legal Marxism and, more generally, of neo-Kantian 'idealism'
on the national scale. His first articles from Vologda (with
the exception of his reportages for *Rabotnik* they are his first
published articles) were attacks on the idealists (9).

Lunacharsky's 'positivist aesthetics' must be seen as a
reaction against the idealists' progressive renunciation of
Marxism and, indeed, of any attempt to explain the ultimate
problems of human existence in scientific terms. His first
attempts to define the nature of art and tragedy are contained
in his polemical reactions to articles by Berdyaev and Bulgakov,
and it is in this context that his grandiose attempt to establish
the principles of a scientific theory of aesthetics and ethics
must be seen. Indeed, at this stage it is only the struggle
against the idealists which gives form and coherence to his ideas.

5. Ermolaev, 'Moi vospominaniya', 5. This is strenuously
denied by another witness. See An. Tarutin, 'K istorii
revolyutsionnogo dvizheniya i politicheskoi ssylki v
Vologde', *Sever*, No. 2, 1924, 3.

6. Lunacharskii, 'Iz vologodskikh vospominanii', 2.

7. Ermolaev, 'Moi vospominaniya', 9; Tarutin, 'K istorii', 3.
Literaturnoe nasledstvo, 82, 618, n. 15.

8. See the entries for 1902-1904 in *Anatolii Vasil'evich
Lunacharskii. Ukazatel' trudov, pisem i literatury o zhizni
i deyatel'nosti*, 2 vols., M., 1975-9, vol. 1.

9. Ermolaev, 'Moi vospominaniya', 8, mentions that Lunacharsky's
first published article, written before his stay in Vologda, was
entitled 'Pedagogicheskie idei Gerbarta'. This article is absent
from the above compendious bibliography.

This is confirmed by his own description of the inception of his system of aesthetics. In the Foreword to 'Principles of a Positivist Aesthetics' he writes:

> Finding everywhere a multitude of elements for the creation of a positivist aesthetics, and realizing how near to a solution of the problem of the Beautiful and its significance many ancient and modern thinkers had come, we were nonetheless not able to find a systematic exposition of the bases of aesthetics which we could pronounce wholly satisfactory. We were obliged to construct a system from the separate parts more or less independently. It is our task not to expound an already existent positivist aesthetics, but to construct it to a considerable extent *ab initio*.(10)

Lunacharsky regarded Marxism not merely as a social doctrine, but as a philosophy of life: 'Combining naturally and harmoniously with the evolutionary and monistic outlook of science, giving it meaning, linking it with the practical questions of life - Marxism was truly a lamp, and the central point of my consciousness' (11). Nonetheless, Darwinism and Marxism, which formed such a harmonious whole, seemed to deal with the individual only externally. While not doubting that ultimately science should aspire to comprehend human life as a 'regular energy transfer process', Lunacharsky felt the need for some theoretical framework for dealing with the phenomenon of human consciousness. Seeking a theory which would not only satisfy his own requirements, but which would also harmonize with Marxism, he 'was fortunate enough to come across the biological theory of cognition of Richard Avenarius and with the views on this subject of Ernst Mach' (12).

No doubt Lunacharsky did see Marxism as a part of the positivist edifice and supposed that the harmoniousness with which the philosophy of Avenarius could be combined with it was a direct result of the positivist base common to both. Nevertheless, one feels sympathy for Berdyaev's taunt that the resulting philosophy was a 'Russian salad of Marx, Avenarius and Nietzsche' (13).

10. Lunacharskii, 'Osnovy pozitivnoi estetiki', in *Ocherki realisticheskogo mirovozzreniya*, SPb., 1904, 114-82. Reprinted in A.V. Lunacharskii, *Sobranie sochinenii*, 8 vols., M., 1963-7, 7, 32-100.

11. Lunacharskii, *Etyudy kriticheskie i polemicheskie*, iii - Foreword.

12. *Ibid*.

13. N.A. Berdyaev, 'Filosofoskaya istina i intelligentskaya pravda', in *Vekhi*, 2nd edition, M., 1909, 16.

While not regarding himself as Bogdanov's pupil,
Lunacharsky acknowledged that he 'learned and developed
in [Bogdanov's] presence and assimilated a great deal from
him'. Bogdanov had from his youth had faith in the
'universal applicability of the elements of Marx's teaching'
to the creation of a general philosophy of life. Lunacharsky
admitted that such universalism was often close to eclecticism,
but considered that Bogdanov's immense application preserved
him from this. Nonetheless, his criticisms of Bogdanov are
applicable to his own theorizing when he notes that Bogdanov's
'monistic instinct' led him to concoct excessively private
systems which, for all their internal consistency, never
commanded widespread recognition (14).

Three days after meeting Bogdanov's sister, Lunacharsky
proposed to her and on 1 September 1902 he and Anna
Aleksandrovna were married. The bride was nineteen and
Lunacharsky was twenty-six (15). The bride was given away
by Bogdanov's colleague at the mental hospital, I.E. Ermolaev,
who, on hearing of Lunacharsky's intention to marry, raised
the question which had plagued Manuel. Ought not a revolutionary
to remain free in order to devote himself body and soul to the
revolution? True to type Lunacharsky replied 'I am very
versatile ...' (16)

But Lunacharsky was not to stay for long in Vologda,
despite Bogdanov's useful placement as a doctor at the
Kuvshinovo Mental Hospital. The Tsar had commanded that
Lunacharsky be exiled to Vyatka, but on 26 December 1902
Nicholas II received a report from the Minister of the Interior,
V.V. Pleve, based apparently on a false medical certificate
engineered by Bogdanov, and instead 'graciously deigned to
command that Anatolii Lunacharsky be permitted to serve the
remaining period of residence under police supervision ordained
by His Majesty's command of 1 May 1902 in the Province of
Vologda' (17). By this time Lunacharsky was becoming a thorn
in the flesh of the Vologda authorities with his boisterous
speeches at public debates and his general activism. Already
by July 1902 he and Boris Savinkov were bracketed together in
a police report as 'Behaving in an unseemly manner. Acquainted

14. Lunacharskii, 'Aleksandr Aleksandrovich Bogdanov', *Pravda*,
10 April 1928, No. 85, 3.

15. *Literaturnoe nasledstvo*, 82, 552, 607.

16. Ermolaev, 'Moi vospominaniya', 9.

17. I.P. Kokhno, 'Vologodskaya ssylka Lunacharskogo', *Literaturnoe nasledstvo*, 82, 607.

with and patronises all those under police supervision' (18).
He was felt to be an unsettling influence on the workers at
the Vologda State Liquor Warehouse, and on 19 February 1903
he was informed of the Governor's decision to move him out
to Tot'ma, over a hundred miles to the north-east and
inaccessible by rail (19). His protests and appeals might
have succeeded had he and Savinkov not been responsible for
sending a delegation of exiles to the Governor to protest
at some infringement, as they saw it, of their rights.
Lunacharsky in particular spoke insultingly of the Governor
at the preceding meeting which was, of course, fully reported
(20). He was sent off to Tot'ma on 23 February. He caught
influenza en route and after a couple of weeks in the intermediate town of Kadnikov took a train back to Vologda, sending
his luggage in advance. This was seized by the police and,
as a result of the inventory taken, we know of what might
otherwise have been another of Lunacharsky's literary works
to disappear without trace. Among the items listed was 'Note-
paper, large format, lined, written upon, on last page thereof
is depicted a human head, drawn in pencil with headdress
resembling a bishop's mitre bearing the legend "Louse"
[Podlets] in capital letters'. Lunacharsky was arrested
and for a week he was incarcerated in the town jail from
8 pm to 10 am daily. The rest of the time he was permitted
to spend at home with his wife and a policeman, who stayed
in the kitchen and passed the time of day with the cook.
Lunacharsky wrote to the police requesting the return of his
papers, but his handwriting having proved indecipherable the
request was turned down for the time being. *The Louse* was
forwarded to St. Petersburg for further study, but there too
the code-breakers were apparently defeated, and a few days
later the Deputy Director of the Police Department returned
the offending document to the Governor of Vologda studiously
avoiding reference to the written content, but noting that
the drawing was evidence of political unreliability and might
justify exile to some yet more remote part of the province.
This was not acted upon. Lunacharsky subsequently requested

18. I.P. Kokhno, *Cherty portreta*, 14, n. 3.

19. *Cherty portreta*, 14, n. 3, 18; *Literaturnoe nasledstvo*, 82, 611.

20. 'Iz vologodskikh vospominanii', 3. N. Panchenko describes
a manuscript bearing corrections and endorsed by Lunacharsky
relating the harrowing story of a servant boy who committed
suicide after being thrown out of school for lack of funds.
He surmises that this may have been what caused Lunacharsky to
fall foul of the Governor. See N. Panchenko, 'Avtografy A.V.
Lunacharskogo v Pushkinskom dome', *Russkaya literatura*, L.,
No. 2, 1966, 213.

the return of:

> certain papers and notebooks comprising the first
> part of my novel *The Louse* prepared for publication
> in a certain monthly journal. In addition to its
> value personally to me this manuscript has a market
> value of 300-400 rubles and is in no way illegal or
> prejudicial in content. I shall read it with pleasure
> to any person the Police care to nominate. (21)

The manuscript was returned, but no more is known of its fate.
Lunacharsky was again sent to Tot'ma but, lacking a necessary
passport-sized photograph, was again detained at the intermediate
town of Kadnikov (22). Sharing a cell with three peasants who
had committed murder he contracted an itch which developed into
erysipelas. When he eventually arrived in Tot'ma the local
doctor suspected blood poisoning and gave him up as a terminal
case, but fortunately the diagnosis proved overly pessimistic
(23).

Although Lunacharsky had no wish to leave the scene in
Vologda, or to tear his young wife away from her family, Tot'ma
proved a far from disagreeable place of exile, and Lunacharsky
even saw it as a mark of consideration that the Governor had
sent him there.

> Tot'ma is an enchanting picturesque little town
> with rococo churches on the banks of a vast river.
> Dark forests stretch away on the other side. Not
> far from the town is a monastery where some wonder-
> working monk lived, and we could travel there through
> the silvery woods of winter on a sleigh. We would be
> offered bread, kvass and fish soup, the like of which
> I never tasted before or since. (24)

Among its population of five thousand, Lunacharsky, the only
political exile, was a celebrity. At first, as he put it, the
local society 'helped me to live, but hindered my work'. He
was planning to start lecturing when a former police sergeant
from Vologda with whom he had crossed swords was promoted
Inspector and transferred to Tot'ma. He managed to frighten
away nearly all Lunacharsky's new acquaintances, thus
releasing him for literary work (25). In just over a year
spent in Tot'ma Lunacharsky wrote a series of lengthy works
on philosophical and literary themes, as well as continuing
his book reviewing. His police report notes approvingly 'He

21. Kokhno, 'Vologodskaya ssylka Lunacharskogo', 613.

22. *Ibid.*

23. Lunacharskii, 'Iz vologodskikh vospominanii', 3-4.

24. *Ibid.*, 4.

25. *Literaturnoe nasledstvo*, 82, 614, 616-17.

lives entirely morally, not dissolutely, and spends his time
in his apartment reading books and newspapers' (26).

Already in Kaluga Lunacharsky had begun writing little
'fantasias' in which in a literary, and hence emotionally
coloured, form he presented various philosophical notions
which appealed to him. He sent a number of these from Vologda
to the Moscow newspaper *Kur'er*,where they were published under
the pen-name of Anatolii Anyutin (Anyuta being, of course, Anna
Aleksandrovna). He continued writing in Vologda, and the
fantasias became noticeably more prickly, clearly alluding to
the polemic with the legal Marxists and in many cases
illustrating points made against them in his lectures and
articles of the time.

Internal evidence suggests that four of the stories
date from Kaluga (the dated manuscripts of some of them may well
be gathering dust in the Party archives). *Moonlight, The
Violinist*, and *The Harp* appeared together late in 1902 (27).
Elements of the Soul was published in *Kur'er* in March 1903.
Moonlight invites interpretation as a self-parody by Lunacharsky
of his slightly ridiculous position in the Goncharov ménage.
The scene is similar to that in *War and Peace* where Prince
Andrei overhears Natasha and Vera chattering as they look out
of their bedroom window at the moonlit garden, but the style
is unmistakably mock-Lermontov. A sad young man looking out
on a moonlit garden hears the loving voices of a man and woman
on the balcony above. The moon shines down dazzlingly.
Everything glistens in the silvery light, the leaves, the pond,
a white wall. At his friend's insistence the man sings an
aria.

> I could not make out the words, but the sounds were
> gentle and profound, and vibrant with a happiness
> which was rapturous, momentarily pensive, but full
> of ardour and awareness of its own heavenly strength.

> Damn! Damn! Damn! Something evil, caustic,
> prickly grows in my breast and rises to my throat.
> A tremor of impatience runs through my body and
> makes me clench my teeth. I want to shout something
> filthy at them, to yell 'Shut up! I'm trying to
> sleep!' I want to swear. I pace the room and
> come back to the window. How fragrant the jasmine
> is. In the pond something splashes quietly beneath
> a marvellous column of shining sparkling silver. (28)

26. *Ibid.*, 616.

27. 'Malen'kie fantazii. Lunnyi svet, Skripach, Arfa',
Russkaya mysl', M., No. 11, 1902, 48-53.

28. 'Lunnyi svet', in Lunacharskii, *Idei v maskakh*, M., 1912,
21-2, 24.

The couple hear his sobs and the young woman considerately has
him sent down a basket of fruit and flowers. Like some
Lermontovian misfit he is only irritated by her happiness and
by the beauty of the scene.

> Take a pistol and suddenly ... bang! What a fright
> they'd get. That would show her what I think of her
> present. A mad answer, but right, right ... (29)

In fact the answer is wrong. In his rejoinder to Berdyaev
Lunacharsky was to elaborate: 'The universe is dreadful in
its non-conformity with our desires [...] no one may stare
for long with impunity into its mindless eyes. This drives
people to the noose, or into dreaming up metaphysical systems'
(30). Unlike the moon-struck narrator, the couple above have
a self-reliant happiness. At the risk of over-resolving
Lunacharsky's symbolism, the basket of fruit and flowers may
be seen as a small 'humanized' part of the universe, artfully
arranged, like the garden itself, like the aria, like the
Goncharovs' 'miniature Athens', so as to be pleasing to man.

Human happiness is the subject also of *The Harp*. A
harp is owned by an old singing teacher who uses it to accom-
pany his pupils. Half the harp's strings he plucks constantly
as he plays the same old tunes, of the others he plucks some
rarely, and some he never plucks at all. But the harp knows
it has these strings. It has stood by the window and the wind
has teased them, prompting a yearning which has never been
satisfied. One day an eminent composer comes to visit his old
friend the music master. He takes up the out of tune harp,
tunes it, and plays his own accompaniment to the *Lamentation
of the Children of Israel* and then the *Song of Songs*.

> And he took me, gathered me in his warm arms. He
> tightened some of my strings. They trembled at the
> touch of his fingers. And suddenly - my god! Is this,
> can this be me? What angelic sighs filled the room,
> What gold, what prayers, what tears. What depths he
> opened [...] So this is music. This is living. So
> this is what those strings can do which I myself was
> all but ready to despise, which were silently atro-
> phying. And what happiness he revealed to me! (31)

29. *Ibid.*

30. 'Tragizm zhizni i belaya magiya' (1902). Reprinted in
Etyudy kriticheskie i polemicheskie, 201.

31. 'Arfa', in *Idei v maskakh*, 38.

The story illustrates a definition of the ultimate human
ideal which Lunacharsky had received from Avenarius in Zurich.
As Lunacharsky defines the ideal mode of existence, 'A
healthy life intensified to the "maximum" is at the same
time the "maximum" of pleasure. This ideal "maximum" would
be achieved where all the organs of a living body, including
the organs of so-called spiritual life, functioned absolutely
correctly, that is, in accordance with their structure' (32).
The harp is a symbol of the human organism. That it achieves
fulfilment and ideal happiness in the hands of an artist is
not without significance.

'An artist is an artist because he understands life more
sensitively and profoundly - he has a right to instruct, Sire!'
(33). So the violinist tells the Emperor of France in The
Violinist. He has succeeded in charming 'this curse of France
and the world, this scourge of God, this genius of extermina-
tion, this fiend' with his playing. The humble servant of
harmony has penetrated the satanic darkness of the Emperor's
soul. Trying his utmost to express through his playing

> the rays of a sunset infinitely sadder and more sacred
> than that which he was contemplating, the song of a
> setting sun, translucent, welling up deeply meditative
> ... It grew and was transformed into a passionate
> religious ecstasy of love and rapture ... And, cut
> off in mid-flight, it broke into stifled sobbing;
> my violin sobbed, trembling, convulsed like a bitterly
> hurt child in the arms of Nature ... like a young man
> on the coffin of his dead bride ... (34)

Having thus prepared the fiend, the violinist ventures to address
him on the need for compassion, on the wrongfulness of causing
needless suffering in a world where life is so short and so
vulnerable.

'What the devil!' the Emperor said at last. 'Are you
a priest or a free-mason? Do you really think I am going to
let you tell me how to lead my life just because I happen to
like your gut-scraping?' (35)

He does, however, let the musician leave.

34. Ibid.

35. Ibid.

32. 'O khudozhnike voobshche i o nekotorykh khudozhnikakh v
chastnosti' (1903). Reprinted in Lunacharskii, Sobranie
sochinenii, 7, 14.

33. 'Skripach'. Reprinted in Idei v maskakh, 20.

time the Emperor is wrong. In 'On the Question of
' (1905) Lunacharsky was to divide human values into
ories, hedonistic, utilitarian, moral, and aesthetic
aesthetic type's commitment is to *joie de vivre*,
nd the striving towards boundlessly increasing
s. It is he who most fully recognises the biologically
given uses of pleasure and value and who, because his love is
for the admired object and its growth rather than for his own
enjoyment of it, overcomes the limitations of egotism. Not
only in artistic, but also in matters of social evaluation, it
is he who is the ultimate arbiter.

In *Elements of the Soul,* published just as Lunacharsky's
carriage was completing the last muddy miles to Tot'ma, the
narrator, dallying near a swamp one still evening, has over-
heard a conversation between three spirits which together
constitute the soul of man (37). They characterize themselves
in discourse - the astral spirit, incorporeal and powerless in
herself, born of starlight and the pure air; the naked woman
on a deer, radiating vigour and cruelty and uttering, Tarzan-
like, cries of lust and rapacity; and finally, apparently
Belial's friend and relative, the god of the swamp himself,
lethargic and mindless. The astral spirit and the woman on
a deer correspond to the unbearable human longing for the
ideal and to human aggressiveness. For Lunacharsky the god
of the swamp represents the urge to abandon public life and
settle down to cosy domesticity. Such is the human inheritance.
But the god of the swamp is present not only within Man, he is
present also in the world of Nature. Perhaps the most daunting
aspect of the stage on which Man has to act is the sublime
indifference of Fate and Nature to his strivings.

Lunacharsky's voluminous published output during his
exile is eloquently expressed, but as analytical writing it
is appallingly bad. Masquerading as philosophy, it might
seem that it would have been better written for the drawer
as a private aid to assimilation of his extensive reading at
this time. In fact, however, his disputations with the legal
Marxists were political rather than philosophical and he later
quite correctly brought the major articles together into
volumes bearing the titles *Critical and Polemical Essays* and
Responses to Life (38). His outlook is less a rational system
of philosophical views (*mirovozzrenie*) than an emotionally
based and polemically advocated system of beliefs and convictions (*mirooshchushchenie*). He himself distinguished two

36. 'K voprosu ob otsenke', in *Etyudy kriticheskie i polemi-
cneskie*, 392-410.

37. 'Elementy dushi', *Kur'er*, M., 27 March 1903, No. 29, 3.

38. *Etyudy kriticheskie i polemicheskie*, M., 1905: *Otkliki
zhizni*, SPb., 1906.

basic temperaments, that of the rationalist and that of the
emotionalist. He unhesitatingly placed himself in the latter
category (39). Accordingly, he often misinterprets his
opponents, and can find no saving grace in any of their
writings. He sees them as the other side in a battle of
cosmic proportions which has been waged for millenia between
the forces of good (biological and social progress) and evil
(biological regression and social reaction). These rather
breathtaking perspectives are evident in his remaining stories
which show precedents in Indian mythology, ancient Greece,
northern Europe in the Middle Ages, China and Italy at the
time of the Renaissance, and in seventeenth-century Holland.
His reading and his imagination are wholly subservient to the
task of discrediting such misguided and harmful cripples, so
that his articles and his stories are much closer than one
might expect.

Berdyaev with his emphasis in *Problems of Idealism* on
the unalterably tragic nature of life gets drastic treatment
in *Princess Turandot* (40). Unable to choose between two
suitors, the Princess decides to marry whichever will prove
his devotion to her by coming to her the next morning with his
ears cut off. If both arrive earless, she will marry whoever
manages the happier smile. The young Mandarin Blue Eyes
(Berdyaev?) decides, after prolonged mental anguish, to comply
with the Princess's monstrous demands and sends for his surgeon.
The other suitor, however, a Venetian who is the secretary of
Marco Polo, disguises himself as a fortune-telling hag,
penetrates into the palace grounds and finding the Princess
in a lonely spot throws off his disguise and forces her to
submit to him. Blue Eyes duly appears earless only to find
that the rules have been changed. The Princess has already
been won by a more 'positive' approach.

Lunacharsky characterises the difference between the
practically inclined revolutionary positivists and the
idealist metaphysicians in terms of Avenarius's views on
the reaction of organisms to a change in their environment.
An organism faced with an alteration in its environment must
either struggle against and overcome the threatening new
conditions, or it must passively adapt to them by regressing
to a lower level of existence.

39. Lunacharskii, Foreword to *Ot Spinozy do Marksa*, M., 1925,
3-5.

40. 'Printsessa Tyurandot', *Kur'er*, No. 27, 1903, 3.

64

>If an organism has been subjected to some new environ-
>mental influence or has been obliged to intensify
>some function (perform work) far beyond its normal
>limits ... it has often two alternatives: the plastic
>- to evolve some complex new reaction to increase its
>powers, or to substitute one kind of reaction for
>another, less habitual, but more economical; or the
>passive - simply to reject the work, to retreat,
>avoid, endure, make do with less.(41)

Where the fatalistic Blue Eyes regresses, symbolically losing
his ears in the process, the Renaissance Venetian resolves the
dilemma by active intervention to change the situation.

A similarly reactionary contemplativeness is discredited
in favour of positivism in *Wings* (42). The setting is again the
Renaissance, a period dear to Lunacharsky for seeing the rebirth
of intellectual enquiry at the expense of religious obscurantism.
In Milan the mystically inclined and physically degenerate
Sicilian physician Pippo Popoloni crosses swords with the handsome young Leonardo da Vinci. Leonardo is just coming to
Darwinistic conclusions about a beetle he is studying in the
dust when he is interrupted by Popoloni who pours scorn on his
empiricism. Reliance on the five senses will never enable him
to rise higher than the dust. He, Popoloni, has just learned
how to fly by reciting sixty times a prayer composed (in
execrable Latin) by a Scottish abbot and taking a swig from
a phial of hallucinogenic fluid. Soaring above Lombardy he
rose last night higher and higher until he could see the disc
of the earth supported in the darkness by God's power. He
flew through one of the holes in the crystal moon to the
second heaven and saw its other side on which is depicted,
not Cain contemplating his slain brother Abel as on the side
visible from Earth, but the Lamb of God with seven ranks of
angels praising him and singing 'Hallelujah'. Tonight he plans
to journey on to the third or fourth heaven in the same trans-
port.

That evening Leonardo goes round to visit him and invite
him to attend an experiment the next day, but finds him already
oblivious on a filthy pile of bedding, the sticky hallucinogen
trickling from his mouth. He makes a sketch of the disgusting
sight and writes underneath 'Even should you ascend to the
seventh heaven you will not escape from the sphere of your
own fancies'. Popoloni will find, not more abundant life,
but only death as he burns out his brain.

41. Lunacharskii, 'Osnovy pozitivnoi estetiki', in Lunacharskii,
Sobranie sochinenii, 7, 37.

42. 'Kryl'ya', *Pravda*, M., No. 4, 1904, 11-16.

The next morning Popoloni, suffering from an excruciating hangover, walks out from the city, darkly apprehending the empirio-criticist truth that, if Leonardo is right and all he saw was but a figment of the mind, then the universe itself is a figment of the mind. By coincidence he stumbles unseen upon Leonardo as he and an apprentice carry out the first modest, but successful, flight of an earthly flying machine.

One of Lunacharsky's later stories, published just after the end of his period of exile but doubtless written in the tranquillity of Tot'ma, is *Charudatta the Wise* (43). Nirvana, the blissful contemplation of God, is what Lunacharsky describes as the 'static' ideal of life negation, the principle of which he considers Berdyaev to be the representative (44). If the submissiveness to fate of Blue Eyes and the obscurantism of Pippo Popoloni were peripheral to this, it is explicitly identified here in a humorously told story set in the realms of Hindu mythology. Charudatta retires after a full and varied life to a cave to contemplate Amtman, the great Nothing. He starves and scourges his body and is duly rewarded with the insight that All is Nothing. Having fifteen times achieved contemplation of Amtman he concludes that the world in which Nothing is clothed is itself remarkably beautiful and interesting, that he personally is becoming stupider, and that Amtman is not life, but death. For this independence of mind Charudatta is rewarded by a vision of Ganesh, the elephant-god of wisdom, who explains to him the harmfulness of contemplation. Man's five senses and his mind have been given to him to be used and it is hardly surprising if, when they are not used, everything seems to be nothing. The world is composed of forces in eternally changing conflict or collusion whose infinite transfigurations certainly do not add up to nothing, neither are they a matter of indifference. It is meritorious for a Rajah to become a Brahmin, but not the reverse. Nevertheless, the future is contained in the present and Ganesh offers to show Charudatta how, like some remote precursor of Marx, he can study the laws by which the world transforms itself, and thereby predict the future.

Charudatta proves brilliantly adept at this. Having with total accuracy predicted for one year drought and rains, victories and defeats of the Rajahs, the loss and increase of cattle, births and deaths, heavenly portents, and the fortunes of traders, he sets out self-importantly and a little sadly into the world with new tables to tell those he meets of what inevitably awaits them in the coming years.

43. 'Mudryi Charudatta', *Pravda*, No. 9, 1904, 29-34. Reprinted in *Idei v maskakh*, 5-16.

44. 'K voprosu ob otsenke', in *Etyudy kriticheskie i polemicheskie*, 409.

In the event he makes a complete fool of himself, since fore-
warned of disaster the Maharajah of Purushri outflanks and
destroys an 'inevitable' ambush; a loving wife kills herself
rather than be guilty of 'inevitable' future infidelity.
Thoroughly ashamed of himself Charudatta curses Ganesh for
his tables which do not work, but is told by the elephant-
god, a forebear evidently of revolutionary rather than
legal Marxism, that he has forgotten to include in his calcula-
tions human consciousness, his own insight and the insight of
those he warns of where the present is leading. If a pit in
the road ahead is pointed out to him a man is not obliged to
fall into it. He may in a panic rush back the way he has come;
overcome with dizziness he may fall into it anyway; but seeing
its finite dimensions he may go forward, taking care not to
fall into it. At this simple solution of the problem of free-
will in a world of historical determinism a weight is taken
from Charudatta's and, let us hope, from the legal Marxists'
shoulders. The tables are indeed infallible, Lunacharsky
asserts. Man is indeed free to master and manipulate the
factors influencing his fate. Man is free, Ganesh tells him,
to order his desires, to decide what his priorities are, and
then, mindful of the drift of things, to go forward in creative
freedom. Whether ultimate tables could be devised to take
human insight into account, that, says Ganesh firmly, is a
secret. It is no concern of man's whether the gods find the
world boringly predictable. Charudatta wakes. It was a dream.
But after a moment's reflection he decides, 'What would a man
be worth who could sit in a cave after such a dream. I shall
go out into the world to struggle for the beautiful things
which can be man's on earth' (45).

        Contemplative submissiveness, the aspiration to nirvana
are forms of 'static' negation of life. There exists however
also a 'dynamic' negation of life, asceticism (46). We have
already met Manuel's superiors with their advocacy of mortifi-
cation of the flesh. In one of Lunacharsky's most Gothic stories,
The Funeral, black figures shuffle through the streets to the
cathedral (47). Occasionally a voice is heard to murmur, 'She
is dead'. Inside the cathedral lies the body of the beautiful
young queen who had abandoned mediaeval Christianity for the
worship of the goddess Freya. She and her people had given
themselves over to a life of joy and physical pleasure. Now
death has ended her reign and the priest drives a stake into
her breast: 'A terrible power reigns in heaven: man's lot is
to tremble, to obey, to flagellate himself, bowed down with
remorse to recognize his wretchedness ... You have forgotten
all this! Oh, we shall teach you!' As the cowering people

45. *Idei v maskakh*, 16.

46. *Etyudy*, 409.

47. Anatolii Anyutin, 'Pokhorony', *Kur'er*, No. 27, 1903, 3.

disperse 'the windows of the College of Priests shone out with
red light and gazed ominously upon the lifeless town' (48).

For Lunacharsky such repression of the emotions can no
longer be justified. He believes that modern man can gain,
through positivism, an adequate understanding of the consequences
of his actions, while his emotions are evolving from blind passion
to a much more complex and graduated system of emotions. 'Man's
task is to gain full control of his reason and delicate sensitivity and bring them into harmony with his will, in order that,
so armed, the will may do battle with the elements, ever closer
to the only true, joyous and positive solution of the eternal
problem' (49).

Lunacharsky's two remaining stories take issue specifically
with another legal Marxist, Sergei Bulgakov, against whom
Lunacharsky also lectured in Vologda, later transforming the
lectures into articles (50). Bulgakov's central contention was
that the Marxists' conception of man was so lacking in compassion as to destroy the ethical momentum essential for a
humane movement for social reform. Was not the price to be
paid in the suffering of today's innocent children too high
for a promise of paradise for the people of tomorrow? (51).
Lunacharsky's reply at the time had been that since socialism
was coming, like it or not, it was no more relevant to ponder
the morality or otherwise of its birth-pangs than to question
whether it was moral for lightning to kill people. He mocked,

> Yes, Mr. Bulgakov's memories of Marxism are vague
> indeed, vague and inaccurate. Wherever did he see
> justification of the present, or buying of the
> future? What we see is the theory of the class
> struggle in accordance with our sympathies.(52)

48. *Ibid.*

49. Lunacharsky's view here seems close to Schiller.

50. The long development of Lunacharsky's polemic against
Bulgakov's interpretation of Goethe's *Faust* is examined in
my article 'Lunacharskii's Russian *Faust*', *Germano-Slavica*
(Waterloo), III, 3, Spring 1980, 189-203.

51. Sergei Bulgakov, 'Ivan Karamazov (v romane Dostoevskogo
"Brat'ya Karamazovy" kak filosofskii tip' [lecture read in
Kiev, 21 November 1901] , *Voprosy filosofii i psikhologii*,
No. 1, 1902. Reprinted in Bulgakov, *Ot marksizma k idealizmu*,
SPb., 1903, 83-112.

52. Lunacharskii, 'Russkii Faust', *Voprosy filosofii i
psikhologii*, May-June, 1902, 783-95. Reprinted in Lunacharskii,
Etyudy kriticheskie i polemicheskie, 183.

In *Smiling Philosopher* Lunacharsky takes us back to ancient
Greece where Democritus is expounding his atomic theory to the
citizens of Abderite (53). Cognition takes precedence over
the sufferings of mankind, he states. And he elaborates his
theory which seems remarkably akin to that of Ganesh:

> 'We can divine the eternal rules of the turbulent
> game of All-Being. If you understand that the
> world's innermost nature is ever-new combinations
> of unchanging matter, you will understand how
> amusing and entertaining life is and will cheer-
> fully take part in the overall game.'
>
> His eyes came to rest affectionately on us.
>
> 'It is as if the world had an urge to satisfy its
> own insatiable curiosity ... Its only concern is
> that things should be interesting. Do you follow
> me? Joy and sorrow are fleeting: with a smile on
> your lips observe. Try to discern in life's ups
> and downs its eternal laws, and ever new per-
> spectives will open up before you.' (54)

As in many of Lunacharsky's stories, the assertion is immediately
put to the test by an incident. A money-lender and his men are
dragging past the defaulting merchant Anastasios and his wife
to be sold into slavery. Anastasios accuses Democritus of the
fault of which Bulgakov accused the Marxists. 'You and your
smiling! You've made everyone pitiless! You don't know what
sorrow is and you've closed the eyes of all those around you
to it ... What could you hold dear, who could you possibly
love?' (55). Democritus with unruffled composure and effort-
less smile gives all his belongings to the money-lender, and
Anastasios is freed. He chides his disciples for praising his
magnanimity. He has saved one individual and now can save no
more, but for the wisdom he dispenses and which can avert
myriad sufferings no one thanks him half so warmly (56).

Here Lunacharsky meets Bulgakov head on. He has no
time for liberal sensitivities. Dostoevsky's innocents are
of no account when weighed against the progress of mankind.
A few months previously he asked rhetorically,

53. 'Filosof, kotoryi smeetsya', *Kur'er*, No. 27, 25 March 1903,
3. Reprinted in *Idei v maskakh*, 40-4.

54. *Idei v maskakh*, 41.

55. *Ibid.*, 43.

56. *Ibid.*, 44.

> Would you really say it would have been better for
> Herod to have killed the infant Jesus and for the
> thousands of infants of Bethlehem to have been
> left alive? When several lives are weighed in the
> scales of justice the matter is settled not by
> quantity but by quality.(57)

The same point exactly is made in 'Spinoza', where the Dutch
philosopher appears to the narrator in a dream, and enmeshing
a noisy fly at his study window in a spider's web watches the
horrifying consequence dispassionately. He turns to the
narrator.

> 'Look,' he said, and pointed his long waxy finger
> at the feast of the spider, 'rejoicing or condoling
> is human, all too human. One must understand ...
> Pain and pleasure are fleeting affects without real
> being ... Understand and love God intellectually'. (58)

What were Lunacharsky's intentions in the writing of
these stories? Because he was dependent for his living on
his writing (and on a subsidy from his mother), were his
motives in part commercial? Just as he re-cycled his Vologda
lectures as articles, so he could further re-cycle the
lectures as fiction. Does the fact that they were published
under a pen-name suggest that they were not intended to make
a major contribution to the polemic against the legal Marxists?
Perhaps they were simply a form of relaxation, of playing with
ideas, and incidentally earning a little extra income? With
their exotic localities they play to Lunacharsky's strengths
as a widely travelled and well-read young man. He dwells
lovingly on the view of the harbour at Abderite from the temple
of Poseidon. He revels in the mediaeval drama of Pippo
Popoloni's visions, or the local colour of Charudatta's
India. At the same time, from the outset his mind seems
made up. The purpose of each story is predetermined, and
Ganesh, Democritus, Leonardo or Spinoza seem all to belong
not only to the supporters of enlightenment in battle against
obscurantism, but indeed to be Marxists of a Bogdanovist
stripe. The setting may be an end in itself, but the story
has no life independent of its moral.

Lunacharsky in fact offered a fairly clear exposition of
the genre of these curious exemplars of political literature.
As an 'emotionalist' (and an experienced orator) he had no
great opinion of the role of rational argument in political
disputation, and in the course of yet another attack on

57. 'Moris Meterlink', *Obrazovanie*, SPb., No. 10, 1902, 148-
67; No. 11, 101-17. Reprinted in *Etyudy kriticheskie i
polemicheskie*, 149.

58. 'Spinoza', *Kur'er*, No. 29, 27 March 1903, 3.

Bulgakov he noted that it was less advantageous to chop logic
with 'idealist' metaphysicians than to mount an attack on the
psychological type of those who preferred poetic metaphysical
systems to an outlook firmly based on empirical reality (59).
In his Vologda and Tot'ma stories it seems clear that he is
carrying on this particular psychological warfare by other,
poetic means.

The work of art differs from the non-poetic work precisely
by affecting the heart, the emotions, and not only reason. Thus
Lunacharsky defined the principal advantage of the tendentious
work of art over the political pamphlet (60). If this observa-
tion is of relevance to his philosophical 'fantasias', it
applies equally to a work of the same type which he substantially
wrote in Tot'ma - *A Dialogue on Art* (61). In the Introduction
Lunacharsky explains the choice of the dialogue form for a discussion on the nature and aims of art:

> I have more than once had occasion to attempt to
> expound my views on art. But a long time ago I
> came to the conclusion that the most suitable form
> for this is that of the dialogue. The dialogue
> enables one to present objectively a number of
> opinions, each one supporting and supplementing
> the others, to build a ladder of views and bring
> them together in one comprehensive idea.(62)

In all likelihood Lunacharsky is indebted for the form of his
'dialogue' to Vladimir Solov'ev's *Tri razgovora* (1900).

The views on art expounded in the dialogue centre
principally around the question of tendentiousness in art, the
argument proceeding as promised in a 'dialectical' manner.
Each speaker represents a definite point of view and takes
up points made by preceding speakers. The last speakers are
Marxists. They summarize and evaluate the preceding discussion,
and give an authoritative statement on the social role of art
which we recognize as Lunacharsky's own view.

The ideas themselves have already been dealt with piece-
meal in Lunacharsky's critical articles. In the primitive

59. 'Idealist i pozitivist kak psikhologicheskie tipy',
Pravda, No. 1, 1904, 118-39. Reprinted in *Etyudy kriticheskie i polemicheskie*, 262.

60. 'O khudozhnike voobshche', in Lunacharskii, *Sobr. Soch.* 7, 9.

61. 'Marksizm i estetika. Dialog ob iskusstve', in *Pravda*,
No. 9-10, 1905, 391-419. Reprinted as 'Dialog ob iskusstve',
in Lunacharskii, *Otkliki zhizni*, 116-63.

62. *Otkliki*, 122.

populist Akinf's denunciation of all art as a plaything and
life-substitute we hear the voice of Veresaev's Osokin, with
whom Lunacharsky took issue in 1903 (63). Boris Borisovich,
the intellectual populist, champions the utilitarian view,
declaring that Homer, Shakespeare and Goethe belong to a lower
category of art, that of 'art-as-play', than Shchedrin and
Uspenskii,whose art is of the 'art-as-preaching' variety.
Skobelev, the bourgeois artist, advocates a Chekhovian artistic
objectivity (64). Erlikh, the decadent, the 'Fichtean mono-
dualist', as he describes himself, puts forward views similar
to those of Berdyaev, which Lunacharsky had attacked, on the
tragic nature of life (65).

Portugez, the first Marxist speaker, gives Lunacharsky's
views on art as a socially cohesive factor, and describes the
link between the cycles of cultural and social history. The
categorizations of class affiliation given above are his. Polina
Aleksandrovna, another Marxist and the last speaker, surveys the
preceding non-Marxist speakers and selects from each a point
with which she is in agreement. Her synthesis is the expression
of Lunacharsky's personal view on the question of artistic
tendentiousness.

Perhaps because of the restriction on space imposed by
the dialogue form, Polina Aleksandrovna's speech is free from
the spurious philosophizing which mars 'Principles of a
Positivist Aesthetics', and the judgements have a pleasing
spontaneity. Despite inadequacies of the dialogue, the form
is justified by the degree of integration which is achieved
in this relatively short, but lively and interesting speech.
D.S. Mirsky, who declared Lunacharsky's plays and verse
'insignificant', found *A Dialogue on Art* interesting (66).
Agreeing with Akinf on the inadequacy of contemporary art
(but adding that he fails to see the dialectic of progress
into which the present may be fitted), agreeing with Boris
Borisovich that the criterion of social utility is of primary
importance in judging art (but substituting for his absolute
a class criterion of a less narrowly utilitarian kind),
agreeing with Skobelev that the artist must be primarily not
a preacher, but an artist, but also agreeing with Erlikh's
insistence on linking art with other human problems,Polina
Aleksandrovna sees the artist at his best as an ally, con-
ceivably unwitting, of the class which most loves life and

63. Lunacharskii, *Sobr. Soch.*7, 7-8.

64. For an attack by Lunacharsky on Chekhov's objectivity see
Sobranie sochinenia, 7, 23-4.

65. See Lunacharskii, 'Tragizm zhizni i belaya magiya', in
Etyudy kriticheskie i polemicheskie, 194-213.

66. D.S. Mirsky, 'A Russian Letter', *London Mercury*, August
1921, 417.

to which the future belongs. In a formula reminiscent of
Chernyshevskii's but, considerably less abrupt than his, she
declares: 'Art is more sublime, the more fully and vividly
it expresses life, and is simultaneously more useful' (67).
But the Chernyshevskian notion of art as a text-book of
life has been dismissed with Boris Borisovich: the emphasis
is on the 'fullness of expression', not on 'life'. The
aesthetic criterion is in a felicitous state of symbiosis with
the social criterion, since aesthetic pleasure begets the
energy needed for social reform. The aesthete draws a lilac
branch and the joys of spring surge through the beholder (68).

In the *Dialogue* Lunacharsky takes stock of the critical
controversies of the recent past, but if he is correct when
he claims it was written in Tot'ma, then there are certainly
later additions (69). The Introduction and ending were
written in 1905, since the Introduction contains a six-page
quotation from a 1905 article by Kautsky and concludes with
a breathless student arriving to announce the government's
abandonment of the Shidlovskii commission of enquiry into
the causes of Bloody Sunday (70).

Into his year in Tot'ma Lunacharsky fitted also the
writing of many reviews for the Moscow journal *Obrazovanie*,
half a dozen polemical articles, the translation of Nikolaus
Lenau's *Faust* and his long article 'Principles of a
Positivist Aesthetics' (71). His stay there was not wholly
idyllic, since his wife fell ill with typhus late in her
pregnancy, with the result that their child was still-born.

Lunacharsky's requests to the Police Department to be
allowed to take a holiday at the seaside to restore his own
and his wife's health were turned down. Anna Aleksandrovna
returned to Vologda for a time (72). Nevertheless he was to
reminisce in 1919:

67. Lunacharskii, *Otkliki zhizni*, 161.

68. *Ibid.*, 160-1.

69. This is stated in the Foreword to the 1919 edition,
reprinted in Lunacharskii, *Sobr. Soch.*, 7, 101.

70. See Lunacharskii, *Sobr. Soch.*, 7, 632, n. 4, where the
quotation is identified as being from K. Kautsky, 'Die
Fortsetzung einer unmöglichen Diskussion', pt. 4:
'Gefühlsozialismus und wissenshaftlicher Sozialismus', *Die
neue Zeit*, No. 49, 29 August 1905.

71. The translation of Lenau's *Faust* is discussed in my
'Lunacharskii's Russian *Faust*', 194-5.

72. *Literaturnoe nasledstvo*, 82, 614-15.

Much as I wrote in Tot'ma, I spent even more time
reading and thinking. Although I had worked assid-
uously enough at Zurich University, and in the
museums and colleges of Paris, I have to admit
that I developed my outlook most successfully
during my eight-month [in fact five-month]
incarceration in the Taganka Prison in Moscow and
the two years [in fact thirteen months] I lived in
Tot'ma.

I never for a moment contemplated trying to escape
from such an exile. I valued the opportunity of
concentrating and of developing my personal
powers. Even so, exile would have been intolerable
had it not been for the wonderful family life which
I enjoyed, and working together with my wife. She
was a close friend who understood everything and a
loyal life-long political companion.(73)

73. *Velikii perevorot*, 28-9.

CHAPTER 5

GENEVA, 1905

On 15 May 1904 Lunacharsky's exile ended, and he and his wife sailed down the river Sukhona to Vologda, where he gave a lecture before travelling on to Kiev (1). Here he wrote theatre reviews for the local newspaper, and a 'popular exposition' of Avenarius's *Kritik der reinen Erfahrung* (2). Lunacharsky's next known fictional writings were written in dramatically different circumstances. His first published poems appeared in *Proletarii*, the weekly newspaper of the Bolshevik fraction of the Russian Social·Democratic Workers' Party.

After the Bolshevik-Menshevik split at the Second Congress of the RSDRP in 1903, Lenin's organizational victory rapidly evaporated. His alliance with Plekhanov foundered and with it his hoped-for control of the Party newspaper, *Iskra*. The Bolshevik-dominated Central Committee, too, opposed his plans to call a third Party congress after winning over a sufficient number of committees within Russia to ensure endorsement of his line. It opposed also his desire to seize back *Iskra* and its printing press 'by revolutionary means'. By the summer of 1904 he had virtually been ousted from the Central Committee (3). Martin Lyadov and others had meanwhile been despatched to Russia to rally the Party committees behind Lenin and, in particular, to round up sympathetic Marxist *littérateurs* who would support

1. *Literaturnoe nasledstvo*, 82, 617.

2. *R. Avenarius. Kritika chistogo opyta. V populyarnom izlozhenii A. Lunacharskogo*, M., 1905.

3. Leonard Schapiro, *The Communist Party of the Soviet Union*, 2nd revised edition, London, 1970, 55-9.

him against *Iskra*'s overwhelming hold on the Party's literary
talent. Lyadov contacted Lunacharsky through Bogdanov:
'Il'ich himself wrote a number of letters in minuscule handwriting on small sheets. Nadezhda Konstantinovna [Krupskaya]
and I also copied out in miniature all the most important
documents. All this was to be concealed in the heel of my
shoe' (4).

Bogdanov came round to Lenin's point of view almost
immediately. He told Lyadov he was sure Lunacharsky, too,
would support Lenin (5). In the event Lunacharsky, returning
to Kiev, heard first from representatives of the Central Committee.
He went to see them in Smolensk (where he wrote a proclamation
for them on the assassination of Pleve), and agreed to collaborate
with them in their campaign to heal rather than exacerbate the
split. But no sooner had he returned to Kiev than he received
a clandestine letter from Bogdanov urging him to join Lenin's
nucleus of Bolshevik writers abroad. Although far from convinced of the rightness of Lenin's position, which was directed
against Lunacharsky's mentors, Aksel'rod and Plekhanov,
Lunacharsky was swayed by Bogdanov's endorsement, and he and
his wife, like some latter-day Manuel and Foletta, after a
brief discussion agreed to set out again on the road of political
emigration (6).

In fact, although Lenin was looking for him in Paris in
mid-summer, it was probably not until October that he arrived,
so missing the Meeting of Twenty-Two Bolsheviks which condemned
the Central Committee conciliators. He went not to Lenin in
Geneva, but to Paris, to Lenin's consternation and even indignation, thus missing even the founding meeting on 29 November
1904 of Lenin's alternative press organ, *Vpered* (7). He was
not finally converted until Lenin came over to Paris to address
a meeting and sought him out.

> One early spring morning [sic] in 1904 there came a
> knocking on the door of my room in the Hotel Lion
> Doré near the Boulevard Saint Germain in Paris. I
> got out of bed. The stairs were still in darkness.
> Before me stood a person I didn't know in a flat hat

4. M.N. Lyadov, *Iz zhizni partii v 1903-1907 godakh.
Vospominaniya*, M., 1956, 27.

5. *Ibid.*, 35.

6. *Literaturnoe nasledstvo*, 80, 738-9; *Velikii perevorot*,
29-30.

7. There is confusion on this point, with Em. Yaroslavskii,
N. Valentinov, the *Bol'shaya sovetskaya entsiklopediya* and
Robert Daniels marking him present at the meeting of Bolsheviks
which took place in July-August. The Introduction to his
popular exposition of Avenarius was, however, signed in Kiev
on 12 September 1904 (O.S.).

and with a suitcase at his feet. To my quizzical
look this person responded, 'I am Lenin. What a
time for the train to get in'. 'Yes,' I said in
some confusion. 'My wife is still asleep. Why
don't you give me your suitcase. We can leave it
here and go and get a coffee somewhere'. (8)

Of this meeting Lyadov recalls, 'Lunacharsky left Russia with
his mind far from made up, but after a short conversation with
Il'ich before his talk, Anatolii Vasil'evich fully appreciated
the significance of the disagreement and spoke out in the
ensuing debate as a convinced Leninist, coping brilliantly
with the Mensheviks and Kadets who spoke against Il'ich' (9).
Lenin's personality evidently settled the matter, for the
time being at least.

Lunacharsky did arrive in time for the second meeting
of the embryonic board of *Vpered*. Ol'minskii, Vorovskii and
Lenin were the other editors. Lunacharsky did not at first
write a great deal as Lenin was most prolific, while Ol'minskii
did most of the rest of the writing. Instead, his rhetorical
skill was exploited and, still following in Manuel's foot-
steps, he toured the Russian colonies of France, Belgium,
Germany and Switzerland championing the Bolshevik point of
view at debates. He also read papers on philosophical and
artistic topics, and confesses that 'they met with incomparably
greater success' (10). Lenin himself was a reluctant orator
and, particularly during 1904 when he had been suffering
from depression, he had made very few public appearances (11).
He therefore encouraged Lunacharsky and would often give him
a preliminary briefing before he set out (12). Krupskaya
recalls that Lunacharsky proved a dazzling orator and contributed a great deal to consolidating the Bolsheviks'
position. The day after his first lecture in Geneva she
wrote in a letter '... now we are all in a better mood thanks
to the arrival of a new comrade - a brilliant orator and
talented writer. He has literally electrified the public.
The Mensheviks are tearing their hair and raising a row ...
the Old Man [Lenin] has perked up and actually seems younger

8. 'Lenin iz krasnogo mramora', 1933, in Lunacharskii,
Vospominaniya i vpechatleniya, 84.

9. Lyadov, *Iz zhizni partii*, 66.

10. *Velikii perevorot*, 32.

11. P.N. Lepeshinskii, *Na povorote (ot kontsa 80-kh godov k
1905 g.)*, 2nd edition, L., 1925, 203.

12. Lunacharskii, 'Opyat' v Zheneve', 2-3. In 1926 he stated
that he 'turn[ed] those slogans which Vladimir Il'ich produced
in abundance into more or less infectious speeches'. Lunacharskii,
'Bol'sheviki v 1905 g.', *Proletarskaya revolyutsiya*, No. 11,
1926. Abridged in Lunacharskii, *Siluety*, M., 1965, 468.

these past few days ' (13). From then on Vladimir Il'ich was
very well-disposed towards Lunacharsky, became gay in his company and was positively partial towards him even during the
period of estrangement from the Vperedists. And Anatolii
Vasil'evich himself was always particularly vivacious and witty
in [Lenin's] company. [...] Lunacharsky, Vorovskii, Ol'minskii
- they were a shot in the arm for *Vpered*' (14).

Lunacharsky overworked himself in the period following
Bloody Sunday (9 January 1905 O.S.) when he was a highly
valued supporter of Lenin. He was active in preparations for
the so-called 'Third' Party Congress which Lenin arranged to
condemn the Mensheviks and new-Iskrites, and, primed by Lenin,
gave a crucial report at it on the question of armed insurrection.
By early June he was suffering from nervous exhaustion and suspected heart trouble, and to Lenin's keen regret went off to
Italy to recuperate (15). Lenin urged him to return.

> The Geneva Bolsheviks are in a wretched state. We
> have a major struggle on our hands. The Third Con-
> gress, of course, did not resolve it, it merely marked
> a new stage in it. The Iskrites are busy as bees, as
> brazen as street-traders, and have the advantage of
> their long experience of demagogy. Our people on the
> contrary are in the main conscientiously stupid (or
> stupidly conscientious). They can't fight, they're
> clumsy, sluggish, awkward, and timid ... Good lads
> all of them - but bloody useless at politics.
> [...] We lack leavening, stimulation, impulsion.
> They can't work or fight on their own. We lack
> speakers at our meetings. There's no one to drum up
> morale, to recognise a matter of principle, to lift
> them clear of the Geneva swamp into the realm of
> interests and topics that really matter. And our
> whole operation is suffering as a result.(16)

Lunacharsky, although flattered, was not to be persuaded. He
replied

> You urge me to come back to Geneva and expect great
> things from my personal intervention. Vladimir Il'ich,
> I remember my 'personal intervention' only too well.
> It was quite nerve-shattering and produced no
> tangible results whatsoever. I felt myself growing
> weak and stupid in Geneva. Here in Italy I am getting
> through an enormous amount of work and building up

13. Quoted in A. Ermakov, *A. Lunacharskii*, M., 1975, 27.

14. N. Krupskaya, *Vospominaniya*, M.-L., 1926, 110.

15. *Literaturnoe nasledstvo*, 80, 4, n. 4.

16. Letter of 20 July/2 August 1905, *Literaturnoe nasledstvo*,
80, 11-12.

physical and mental reserves which I shall des-
perately need when we can finally get back into
Russia.(17)

Although Lunacharsky was active in sending material for the
Bolshevik newspapaper (*Proletarii* succeeded *Vpered* just after
the Third Congress),he was devoting himself primarily to the
study of art history and Italian literature (18). 'My instinct
for spiritual self-preservation cries out against Geneva all
the more strongly because I can feel myself growing inwardly
here' (19).

From Florence Lunacharsky sent four poems to Lenin for
Proletarii. In all he contributed a further twenty-one articles
before the last issue in November 1905. Two of the poems
('Khilkov and the Railway Workers' and 'Witte and the Railway
Workers') have never been published and are presently secure
in the Central Party Archive (20). Lunacharsky mentions a
poem in a rather arch letter to Lenin of 14/27 July 1905.

My friend [doubtless Anatolii Anyutin] has sent
me a poem which I am sending on to you today. Anyuta
liked it so much she suggested I pass it off as my own
over the signature of Voinov [the pseudonym with which
Lunacharsky signed his articles in *Vpered* and *Proletarii*]
If you like it too, please print it in *Proletarii*.
In any case, please send it whether you use it or not
to Bonch for his anthology.(21)

A little later he enquired how Lenin had taken to the poem, and
a few days later he again enquired whether Lenin would be
printing it, urging that, if not, it be sent on to Bonch-
Bruevich (22).

17. Letter of 21 July/3 August 1905, *Literaturnoe nasledstvo*,
80, 15-16.

18. *Velikii perevorot*, 34.

19. *Literaturnoe nasledstvo*, 80, 16.

20. Central Party Archive, Institute of Marxism-Leninism,
Moscow, file 25, schedule 1, item No. 3, part 2, sheets
45-8. Mentioned in *Literaturnoe nasledstvo*, 80, 516, n. 57.

21. V. Perova, *Pered rassvetom. Sbornik revolyutsionnykh
pesen i stikhotvorenii*, Geneva, 'Iskra', 1905. Martov published the anthology, of which he had had the draft since
1903, without Lunacharsky's poem and without further con-
sulting the Bolsheviks: *Literaturnoe nasledstvo*, 80, 8, n. 4.

22. *Ibid*, 14, 24.

Almost certainly Lunacharsky is enquiring about the fate of his poem *In Commemoration of the Ninth of January* (23). He need not have worried. Receiving it Lenin wrote on it 'Print in No. 12 without fail', but in the event it missed the issue of 3/16 August, appearing in No. 13 on 9/22 August (24).

It had been Lunacharsky who first broke the news of the 'Bloody Sunday' shootings to Lenin as he was on his way with Krupskaya to the library in Geneva. Krupskaya recalls that they were seized not only with profound indignation, but also by a realization of the tremendous jolt which the ninth of January would give to the whole workers' movement, and of the immense responsibility which was laid on the Party (25). Lunacharsky claimed that the Bolsheviks now saw the Party as 'the military organisation of the Revolution' (26). Lunacharsky spoke after Martov at the mass meeting called by the RSDRP in Geneva (27).

Within two months of the shootings he had written a substantial pamphlet, *The Workers of Saint Petersburg Go to the Tsar*, which was sent out with *Vpered* No. 13 of 23 March/5 April 1905 (28). In the pamphlet he emphasizes the good intentions, but naivety, of Father Georgii Gapon, who led the workers' march to the Winter Palace. (Through Lenin, Lunacharsky met Gapon in Geneva in mid-February 1905) (29). He emphasizes too, in dialogue form, the lack of illusions among the Social Democratic workers in St. Petersburg regarding Gapon's faith in the Tsar: 'The social democrats kept on repeating their warning: "The Tsar won't come out to you. You'll be shot. If you want to march, then let's go armed!" But Gapon didn't want this and instead ...' (30). He spells out the basic Social-Democratic demands for political progress and shows how these were at least incorporated into Gapon's petition to the Tsar, and how Gapon insisted that weapons and red banners be

23. 'K yubileyu 9 yanvarya', *Proletarii*, Geneva, No. 13, 1905, 3-4.

24. *Literaturnoe nasledstvo*, 80, illustration facing p. 506.

25. N.K. Krupskaya, 'Pamyati Anatoliya Vasil'evicha Lunacharskogo', *Vestnik Kommunisticheskoi akademii*, No. 1, 1934, 81; see also Krupskaya, *Vospominaniya*, 99.

26. *Velikii perevorot*, 34.

27. P.N. Lepeshinskii, *Na povorote*, 216-17.

28. V. Voinov[ps.], *Kak peterburgskie rabochie k tsaryu khodili*, Geneva, 'Vpered', 1905.

29. Lunacharskii, *Vospominaniya i vpechatleniya*, 105-6, 351 n.

30. Reprinted in *Literaturnoe nasledstvo*, 80, 554.

concealed until the Tsar had had his chance. His purpose in
the pamphlet is to persuade his readers of the Bolshevik view
that, peaceful demonstrations having been shown to be hopelessly inappropriate, it is time to prepare for imminent armed
insurrection. He contrasts Gapon's conciliatory attitude before
the demonstration with the proclamation of the 'courageous
priest' dated midnight, 9 January 1905, in which Gapon speaks
of the Tsar-beast and his robber officials, and of the bullets
of the Tsar's soldiers which instantly killed three hundred
workers and, shooting holes in the portrait of the Tsar, killed
the people's trust in the Tsar. Calling for a general strike
Gapon wrote, 'I permit you to take the food to feed yourselves,
your wives, and your children wherever you may. Bombs,
dynamite - I permit everything' (31). Lunacharsky calls, too,
for the setting up of revolutionary committees in the country-
side, which are to usurp the functions of officialdom, but to
avoid unnecessary bloodshed. In his poem Lunacharsky
devastatingly dramatises his pamphlet.

Anticipating Gor'kii's *The Mother*, he takes as his hero
an ideologically backward old worker who personifies Gapon's
naive supporters and who, subsequently, learns the Social-
Democratic truth the hard way. The old man struggles with
his young son to the front of the crowd when Cossacks bar
the marchers' route in order to reason with their General.
Like the real marchers he has total faith in the inviolability
of the icons and portraits of the Tsar. The Cossacks' threats
can only be bluff. How could Orthodox Christians raise their
arms to fire at an icon? God himself would instantly avenge
the sacrilege. He leads the crowds forward. The Cossacks
fire. The old man falls dying, surrounded by blood and confusion. The shattered icons lie in the snow. He sees the
bright sky looking down with soulless cheeriness 'on the
monstrous spectacle and in an instant recognises that neither
God nor the accursed Tsar are any friends of ours' (32). With
his last breath he urges his son to go forward to win freedom
for the workers.

Half a year passes. The son has grown up fast. He
sombrely awaits the hour of insurrection.

Мы не иконы понесем,   This time no icons we shall bring,
Пойдем мы не с портретом,   Not with a portrait we shall come.
А бомбы, ружья, динамит   Our bombs and guns and dynamite
Вам загремят ответом!   Will answer you with thunder.

31. *Literaturnoe nasledstvo*, 80, 556.

32. 'K yubileyu 9 yanvarya', 4.

И не хоругвь над головой	No banner woven in cloth of gold
Завеет златотканный.	Will flap above our heads.
Мы знамя красное взовьем,	The red flag then we shall unfurl,
Великий стяг наш бранный ...	Our glorious battle standard.

(33)

The disillusionment is complete. 'We'll leave the heavens to sparrows, But we'll conquer the earth', and in place of psalms the *Marseillaise* will ring out (34).

One further poem was published in the 14/27 September issue of *Proletarii*, a parody of Heine's *Zwei Grenadiere* with the title *Two Liberals* (35). In the wake of the Tsar's agreement, in August 1906, to a consultative Duma, one of the issues in the Bolshevik war against *Iskra* became the question of the future relationship of the social democrats and the liberals. Lunacharsky was working on an article which sought to draw parallels between the paradoxical political powerlessness of the organizationally very powerful German social democrats (as analysed by Rudolf Hilferding) and the collaborative proposals of Parvus and Martov. As Lenin subsequently put it in an editorial letter to Lunacharsky about his article, the proletariat's strength lay in its revolutionary activism, while that of the Constitutional Democrats lay in a quasi-Parliament. Accordingly, the Menshevik proposals for cooperation with the Constitutional Democrats would barter real power on the streets for a mere semblance of power in a parliament (36). In his 'ballad' Lunacharsky emphasises the incompatibility of liberal interests with those of the proletariat. The leading Kadets I.I. Petrunkevich and E.N. Trubetskoi have been to the Tsar to seek constitutional reforms. Although he has since somewhat gone back on his word, they are confident that with the growth of social unrest he will come to his senses.

Хоть страшно и земцам анархии взрыв,	Though zemstvos too fear the anarchist's bomb
Но трону страшнее он вдвое,	For the throne it is quite doubly fearful.
И, только союз меж собой заключив,	And only uniting ourselves in a deal
Мы властвовать можем в покое.	Can we wield our shared power as securely.

(37)

33. *Ibid.*

34. *Ibid.*

35. 'Dva liberala (ballada)', 4.

36. *Literaturnoe nasledstvo*, 80, 739-40.

37. 'Dva liberala', 4.

The liberal striving for a constitution is merely an attempt to establish oligarchy in place of monarchy, the fundamental structure of exploitation remaining unaltered. Once in power, in accordance with Hilferding's hypothesis, they will deal summarily with 'unrestrained persons' in a properly European manner. And Lunacharsky does not forget in his last verse to put a sting in the tail:

Не бойся же, княже! Не пал либерал
От царственной лжи безобразной, -
Я даже и в "Искре" на днях прочитал:
"Власть будет всегда буржуазной!"

'Fear not, *O mon prince*! Though the Tsar took a crack
With his lies at our fine legislature.
Why even in *Iskra* I read some days back,
"Power will always be bourgeois in nature".'

Lunacharsky's journalism from afar came to an abrupt end. The Tsar's 'Manifesto' of 17/30 October 1905 granting a range of civil liberties resulted in a flood of returning émigrés. Lunacharsky received a telegram from the Central Committee instructing him to return to St. Petersburg, which he did the following day (39).

38. *Ibid.*

39. *Literaturnoe nasledstvo*, 80, 739-40

CHAPTER 6

ST. PETERSBURG, 1905-7

Lunacharsky was to remain in Russia from early November 1905 until February 1907. In terms of political activity he advanced from the abstract theorising of his time in exile, through a year of the factional strife of emigration, directly into the turmoil of the 1905 Revolution and its aftermath. He continued nevertheless to think of himself as a poet and a philosopher, and was later to write of his political work in 1905-7 in terms reminiscent of his letter to Lenin from Florence, almost as if it had been a distraction from more enduring concerns (1).

The civil rights granted by the October Manifesto allowed the Social Democrats to write in legal newspapers. They moved in on, and took over, *Russkaya gazeta* and Minskii's *Novaya zhizn'*. On 26 November Trotsky, Parvus and the Iskrites began publication of the openly Social Democratic newspaper *Nachalo* (2). The 'taking over' of *Novaya zhizn'* from the Symbolist poet N. Minskii and his literary associates, who included such significant writers as Gor'kii, Konstantin Bal'mont, Teffi, Georgii Chulkov, Leonid Andreev, and Evgenii Chirikov, was a messy business which succeeded only because Minskii could not bring himself to have the paper closed down at such a momentous time (3).

Lunacharsky was put in charge of the section surveying the press, and managed also to write an article and two

1. *Literaturnoe nasledstvo*, 82, 553.

2. L. Martow[ps.], *Geschichte der russischen Sozial-demokratie*, Berlin, 1926, 142-3.

3. N. Minskii[ps.] , 'Istoriya moego redaktorstva', in Minskii, *Na obshchestvennye temy*, SPb., 1909, 197-8.

leaders before the newspaper was in any case closed down on
3/16 December (4). In the first half of 1906 he contributed
much purely political journalism to its Bolshevik successors,
Volna, *Vpered*, and *Ekho*, each of which in turn arose from the
ashes of its predecessor. The social democratic political
organizations were weak and Lunacharsky saw the Party press
as having a particularly important role to play.

> They were purely Party newspapers, edited one-
> sidedly, but nonetheless energetically and vigorously,
> and they were very well received by the masses. But
> by the time they came on the scene the superiority of
> a reactionary government over the forces of the Soviet
> was unmistakable. Soon the first Praesidium was to be
> arrested, and then the second headed by Trotsky. (5)

Lunacharsky himself was arrested soon after the failure of the
Moscow workers' armed uprising. On 31 December 1905 O.S. he
was present at a gathering of members of the Social Democratic
organization of the Neva region of St. Petersburg when the
building was surrounded by two companies of the 96th Omsk
Infantry Regiment and the fifty-four participants were arrested
(6). Lunacharsky was imprisoned for a month in the Kresty
prison (which boasted a good library) and wrote an anti-Tsarist
play in blank verse, *The King's Barber* (7). Begun on 9 January
the play was completed in draft within a week and the fair copy
was completed on 25 January 1906, three days before his release
from prison (8).

The King's Barber is, in spite of its loose construction,
one of the most ingeniously conceived of all Lunacharsky's many
plays. The ageing King Dagober the Cruel has decided to probe
once again the limits of his power: he will publicly marry his
own daughter with the Church's blessing and the acquiescence of
the nobility. He will achieve this supreme act of arrogant
self-indulgence by manipulating the interests of various factions
within the Court and the Church. Lunacharsky clearly suggests
a link between Dagober's exploitation of dissension within the
state and the mechanics of tsarism: in a state in which self-
interest is the supreme principle the leader is a referee with
a vested interest. We have already noted Lunacharsky's scorn

4. N.A. Trifonov, 'Lunacharskii v gorode Lenina', *Zvezda*,
L., No. 11, 1965, 183.

5. *Velikii perevorot*, 35-6.

6. A.V. Plavnik, 'Pervye shagi budushchego narkoma', *Neman*,
Minsk, No. 8, 1968, 177.

7. *Korolevskii bradobrei*, SPb., 1906. Quotations are from
Lunacharskii, *P'esy*, M., 1963, 37-129.

8. Information communicated by Irina Lunacharskaya;
M. Gor'kii. Neizdannaya perepiska, M., 1976, 13, n. 1.

for compromise as a political technique. Here the negotiations are concentrated in an act where the Magnates' Council is to deliberate upon the King's proposed unnatural marriage. The King threatens to stir up a popular rising against the nobility if they do not agree to his demands, but promises to lead a campaign against free-thinking landowners, with a general sharing our of the booty, if they agree. The stick and the carrot are too much and they agree. The sole dissenting voices are those of the Chancellor, who fears the King is insane and a threat to the structure of the state, and that of the Mayor of the capital, a medieval left-wing social democrat, who, as the people's representative speaks out against what is repugnant to a humane sense of justice.

Lenin viewed the play with favour and according to Lunacharsky, saw in it 'an attempt, on the one hand, to analyse the nature of monarchic power and the social contradictions on which it rests, and, on the other hand, to show its natural corollary, monstrous power-drunkenness leading to a singular form of insanity'(9). A similar view is expressed by V. Monyukov who finds the play 'actually an allegory of Russian tsarism, unmasking the rottenness and venality of monarchy and showing the inevitability of its downfall' (10). Dagober instructively falls short of embodying Lunacharsky's ethical ideal. Interestingly enough V. Ashmarin in a confused review of 1919 saw Dagober as a positive hero: 'His duality, his attraction to his double the barber, in whom the muck and filth of the criminal elements in man are concentrated, only throw into relief the charm and heroism of the human personality when it has raised the banner of rebellion' (11). To be sure Dagober is an aesthete and pleasure-seeker, and Lunacharsky saw aesthetic evaluation as the criterion for ethical judgements. Manuel in *Temptation* could not conduct his moral and social crusade unless he was physically fulfilled and Lunacharsky saw nothing wrong with the aggressive pursuit of pleasure as such (although Dagober clearly takes it to grotesque lengths). In the philosophical dispute with the neo-Kantians Lunacharsky had to a large extent shared their interest in eschatological problems and consequently in the problem of human mortality. Rejecting their metaphysical-religious solution in favour of a social solution he could overcome the problem of mortality only by denying any absolute value to the individual *per se*. *The King's Barber* expresses this death-based rejection of Renaissance individualism with all the imaginative power Lunacharsky

9. *Literaturnoe nasledstvo*, 80, 230.

10. V. Monyukov, 'Pokazyvali sevastopol'tsy', *Sovetskaya kul'tura*, No. 19, 1961, 3.

11. *Izvestiya*, No. 3, 4 January 1919, 4.

could muster: the individual human organism is mortal, and
therefore cannot embody an absolute.

The action takes place in the 15th century in a feudal,
West European state (12). We hear of heretical free-thinkers
in the state, of painters flourishing in Florence. Dagober is
the cynical, cunning Prince of the Renaissance, exploiting the
divisions of his opponents to raise himself above them. He has
chosen to raise the humble Aristid to be virtually his companion
because he finds him 'depraved, lecherous, shameless, greedy,
inquisitive, a sneak - in fact, a pearl' (13).

> ... Why, then, in secret,
> In foolish dreams which you yourself acknowledge
> As folly, you dare to trample ... all.
> What hold you sacred? What beyond your grasp?
> For this I love you. If you were
> A king, then it might be in truth
> That you would bear some likeness to myself. (14)

Lunacharsky has gone back far beyond Nietzsche and Dostoevskii
to the Renaissance for the very beginnings of the concept of
the Man-God. God has fallen from heaven: Dagober is the
humanists' God:

> King   I'm God on earth, how say you, Aristid?
>
> Aristid   Is there a God in Heaven? - I know not.
>
> King   And so pray in your heart
>   To the great and goodly God
>   Whom now you shave ...   (15)

But Aristid, instead of praying to the God he shaves, aspires,
reasonably enough, to the state of Man-Godhood himself:
arrogating to himself God's sway over life and death, he cuts
Dagober's throat while shaving him on his wedding morning.

> Aristid   I - God of Gods, the destiny of destinies,
>   power
>   Over power! Oh, ecstasy! ...   (16)

12. *P'esy*, 39.

13. *Ibid.*, 125.

14. *Ibid.*, 50.

15. *Ibid.*, 126.

16. *Ibid.*, 128.

The King's Barber is primarily a polemic against individualism. Part at least of the play's power comes from the imaginative treatment of the relationship between King Dagober and the youthful Princess Blanka, who is torn between filial devotion, desire and repugnance towards a union with her own father. In a climactic scene the Princess collapses into insanity and the King is left behind to brood over the miserable triumph of dragging a drugged and mindless daughter to his bed, while his manservant Aristid sings of the gallows, and a dog is heard nearby, baying (17). The style is purest Maeterlinck.

One critic has astutely observed: 'Lunacharsky's first play [sic] was very close formally to the aestheticist-symbolist excursions into the Middle Ages and the Renaissance. It differs from them, however, in its acute socio-political tendentious- ness' (18). Lunacharsky's play indeed exploits Maeterlinck's form specifically for the purpose of polemicising against such 'aestheticist-symbolist excursions'. The mechanism is to counter the individualistic ideal of purist aestheticism with religious insight, and the result is effective and condemnatory. The individual in isolation can aspire to nothing higher than the insane sexual extremism of Dagober. The individual is easily manipulated by the strong-willed parasite. The individual is destroyed by death. Only in the collective will of the people can principles prevail over individual self-interest.

Despite superficial untidiness the play possesses an underlying unity. Lunacharsky sketches in various extraordinary characters who, from a strictly narrative point of view, are clearly not essential. But in the Scottish mercenary, Chaucer, who would serve up the holy relics as a soup in return for an earldom and absolution, or in the pathetic holy woman, Dorothea, who sees visions of a youthful and virile Christ, and in the Princess Blanka's attraction to depictions of the handsome young St. George, there is evident a knack for vivid, even grotesque, characterization developing the one recurring theme of the unreliability of the perceptions and principles of the individual organism. For this reason the contemporary criticism that 'the author does not trust himself as an artist and so overemphasizes his contentions, almost to the point of pulping them, constantly returning to

17. This parody was later published 'straight', set to music by B. Karagichev, as *Pesenka Aristida*, in Karagichev, *Romansy*, SPb., 1912.

18. S.S. Danilov, *Ocherki po istorii russkogo dramaticheskogo teatra*, M.-L., 1948, 516.

them and adding more detail' is not wholly justified (19).
The reviewer in *Vesy* went further and declared that 'all in
all the structure is absurd, the play is drawn out exhaustingly,
and the versification is murderous' (20).

The play does suffer from cerebrality: its lengthy mono-
logues fatigued the audience when it was performed in 1919 (21).
But if it is too long, it is leavened, as are few of Lunacharsky's
other works, with refreshing wittiness; and it achieves a few
very dramatic situations, for example the scene where Dagober
broods on his wretchedly inadequate victory, the scene in the
cathedral where the unhappy and confused Dorothea lies to the
people at the bidding of a Church ruled by selfish men, or the
final scene of Aristid's gruesome apotheosis over the corpse
of his 'God'. N. Balashova spoils an otherwise enlightened
review of a production in Vladimir in 1968 by interpreting
Dorothea as a facile hypocrite. This is a common Soviet interpretation which is clearly at variance with Lunacharsky's
intention (22). To see the superficiality of the characterization as a defect would be to apply a criterion inappropriate to
the genre: Lunacharsky's characters are not intended to be con-
vincing human beings. They are Lunacharskian 'images', illustrating an ideological, or, as he might have argued, a religious
thesis. If we take the play on this level, it is indeed an
engaging and successful effort. Lunacharsky himself described
it as a work 'dedicated to the socio-psychological tasks which
now, in our view, confront Marxist thought' (23). In other
words, a hatchet job on liberal individualism.

Although the play was published in 1906, the rapid
regaining of control by the government made its production
problematical. Lunacharsky wrote to Gor'kii, whom he had
evidently met while working at *Novaya zhizn'*, asking his advice
on how to ease it through the stage censorship. 'I had enter-
tained no hope of seeing it performed on the stage, but I am
glad to say that a number of entrepreneurs have approached me
with proposals, among them, in most flattering terms, N.N.

19. Vl. Kr[anikhfel'd], Review in *Mir bozhii*, No. 6, 1906,
Section 2, 64.

20. A. Kursinskii, *Vesy*, No. 9, 1906, 70.

21. V. Ashmarin, *Izvestiya*, No. 3, 4 January 1919, 4.

22. N. Balashova, 'Bichuyushchii zhestokost' i zlobu',
Teatral'naya zhizn', No. 16, 1968, 15.

23. *Otkliki zhizni*, vii.

Mikhailovskii' (24). He wrote, too, in a hitherto apparently undeciphered letter to Nikolai Aleksandrovich Popov,

> Dear Sir,
>
>   This summer in Finland I had the pleasure of making the acquaintance of N.N. Mikhailovskii, who spoke of you very warmly. I have read and heard in the press [sic] masses of compliments about you as a producer and as a person. Finally even *Teatr i iskusstvo* writes that your theatre must of necessity rely on a semi-proletarian audience. All these things have prompted me to write you this letter.
>
>   N.N. Mikhailovskii has assured me that my first [sic] play, *The King's Barber*, is admirably suited to the stage. The newspaper *Rech'* stated in a notice devoted to my play that 'We need have no doubts at all that the play will be a success on the stage'.
>
>   I propose the following arrangement to you, dear sir. You will take it upon yourself to pilot the play through the Stage Censorship, if necessary at the price of losing a few feathers from its tail.
>
>   I accord you exclusive production rights for the entire season on entirely straightforward terms (i.e. at the standard fee), with the proviso that you share this privilege with N.N. Mikhailovskii and, possibly, with a certain Odessa enterprise (I don't remember the names) as I promised a certain Odessite (Zeilaue) to allow him to stage my play in Odessa, if it were passed by the Censor's Office ...
>
> (25)

In the same letter Lunacharsky assures Popov that he can guarantee that the play will be of interest to the student public. Two thousand of the three thousand people before whom he has delivered one of his lectures heard it at the University and in further education institutions.

        Apparently the 'normalisation' of the country's political life soon put paid to all hopes of a production. Indeed, even

24. Letter written before August 1906, *M. Gor'kii. Neizdannaya perepiska*, 13. Mikhailovskii was the son of the critic, N. K. Mikhailovskii, and an actor and entrepreneur working in 1901-10 with the Nezlobin company in Riga (*ibid.*, 14, n. 6).

25. TsGALI, file 837, schedule 1, item No. 210.

distribution of the text evidently became impossible, since
the play was next to re-appear in a clandestine edition in
1911. On 9 March 1912 the Moscow Press Committee drew the
attention of the St. Petersburg Press Committee to a curious
publication titled *Tales, Short Stories, and Poems. Very
Readable (Povesti, rasskazy i stikhotvoreniya. Chitayutsya
s uvlecheniem)*, allegedly appearing in its fourth edition.
On closer investigation this proved to contain an untitled
brochure and a play, *The King's Barber*, both by unidentified
authors (26). The publication was banned. The Committee
advised that 'the second part of the book contains a play,
The King's Barber, in which the author attempts to demonstrate
the moral turpitude of the bearer of supreme power, in this
case the mythical King Dagober the Cruel. He uses his power
exclusively in the service of his passions; in some parts of
the play, moreover, the author causes the King to give
utterance to blasphemous speeches, for example on pages 13
and 17' (27). The St. Petersburg Court of Justice subsequently confirmed the ban on the publication, but abandoned
the case owing to inability to discover the guilty parties.
The *faute de mieux* decision to destroy all copies of the
offending publication could not be implemented since not a
single copy could be located. In its printed form the play
had managed to appear.

    The King's Barber was to be reissued after the October
Revolution and was frequently produced. Lunacharsky even
wrote a film script from it, although the film was never
made (28). The play is still a pillar of the repertoire of
the Lunacharsky Theatre in Sevastopol.

    While Lunacharsky was in prison, Maksim Gor'kii visited
his wife and took away the manuscript of a play *From Another
World (Iz mira inogo)* (29). The play concerns conflict between
workers and members of the pseudo-revolutionary intelligentsia
and may be based on some of Lunacharsky's misgivings about the
Vologda exiles. It continues to gather dust in the Central
Party archive, and is said to contain some good scenes, but
to be in general bitter, hard-hitting and not in Lunacharsky's
usual style (30). At all events, Gor'kii evidently decided
not to publish it for him.

26. The brochure was M.A. Reisner's *Russkii absolyutizm i
evropeiskaya reaktsiya*, SPb., 'Delo', 1906, 102 pp.

27. V.N. Foinitskii, 'A.V. Lunacharskii i tsarskaya
tsenzura', *Russkaya literatura*, L., No. 4, 1975, 146.

28. Announced in *Pravda*, No. 239, 19 October 1927, 8.

29. Letter from Lunacharsky to Gor'kii, before August 1906,
in *M. Gor'kii. Neizdannaya perepiska*, 12.

30. Information communicated by Irina Lunacharskaya.

Lunacharsky appears to have been fully aware of the purely negative nature of *The King's Barber*, since he refers in 1906 to his plan to produce a related drama representing the growth of 'the most subtle and beautiful impulses in so-called "vulgar" hearts in the atmosphere of the fraternal struggle for the people's rights' (31). He wrote to Gor'kii,

> The notable success of my *Barber* has encouraged me to embark upon a further play in the same style. Its conception is much more comprehensive; its title is *Forebears* and its heroes are the 'common' people. If those nearest to me warmly applauded the first reading of the *Barber*, the first reading of three acts of my new play caused a sensation. I should very much like my new work, which I also view with some favour, to be published by *Znanie*. But once again speed is of the essence. (32)

But *Forebears* was to share the fate of *From Another World*, and has only recently had the dust of the Central Party Archive blown from it.

> As far as the organizational side was concerned, matters were not going particularly well. We and the Mensheviks were both equally aware that the Petersburg Soviet of Workers' Deputies was founded more on a temporary enthusiasm of the workers than on real political consciousness, or more specifically on a real, solid grassroots organization.
>
> At that time Dan was energetically advocating the setting up of a network of clubs, which here and there did get off the ground. Purely Party organizations, the professional organizations, were undeniably still decidedly rickety. As always we were short of people.(33)

So wrote Lunacharsky after the October Revolution. He evidently took Dan's point. He was later closely involved in the beginnings of the Proletarian Culture movement with its network of amateur arts workshops, and in 1906, encouraged no doubt by the success of *The King's Barber*, he wrote *Five Farces for Amateurs* (34). He wanted to provide 'easily produced plays of a comic nature which would meet the demand, which was already becoming apparent at that time, for all

31. *Otkliki zhizni*, vii-viii.

32. *M. Gor'kii. Neizdannaya perepiska*, 13.

33. *Velikii perevorot*, 36.

34. *Pyat' farsov dlya lyubitelei*, SPb., 1907.

sorts of club and amateur performances' (35).

The setting for all these farces is contemporary and
realistic, even prosaic. I.P. Kokhno remarks that the *Five
Farces for Amateurs* abound in details and allusions which
made them highly topical. The polemical talent of Voinov
makes its mark forcefully in them' (36). They attempt to
impart some basic message or insight into the workings of
the old society, or the soul of its opponents. Lunacharsky
characterized their theme as 'socio-political' (37). The
plays are not artistically ambitious, and in general only
show that Lunacharsky was right in later years when he
refused to 'write down for the masses'. He himself did not
have a high opinion of them. They were well enough received
when he read them at various functions to raise money for
political purposes, but he soon became disillusioned with
them and never considered that they merited reprinting in
later years (38).

A farce which continues the polemic of *The King's
Barber* against the more exotic excesses of individualism
is *The Superman* (39). Published a year before Burtsev's
unmasking of the 'Russian Judas', Azef, Lunacharsky's farce
satirizes a figure of perverse spirituality who sees his
achievement in life as lying in the fact that:

> I have carried on a subtle, an artistic game;
> I have deceived everybody because there hovered
> before me a grandiose ideal. I felt strength
> in myself; I was destined to rise high - no
> matter on whose shoulders, no matter over whose
> corpses - but to power! Nothing seemed impossible
> to me. Power, vitality!' (40)

Like Nietzsche's Superman, Roman Panibratov is beyond good
and evil. Modelling himself on a rather Raskol'nikovian
Napoleon he spurns petty morality, declaring that a great

35. Lunacharskii, 'Predislovie k dramolettam' [1930],
published by I.A. Sats, *Teatr*, No. 2, 1966, 75.

36. I.P. Kokhno, 'Dorevoyutsionnaya dramaturgiya
A.V. Lunacharskogo', *Uchenye zapiski Karel'skogo ped.
instituta*, Petrozavodsk, 18, 1967, 31.

37. Letter to N.A. Popov, 1906, cited in note 25 above.

38. 'Predislovie', *Teatr*, No. 2, 1966, 75.

39. 'Sverkhchelovek', in *Pyat' farsov dlya lyubitelei*, 3-24.

40. *Pyat' farsov*, 21.

man's duty is to himself alone. The practical expression
of his freedom is that he acts as a provocateur for the
police. Although married, he lives with a mistress who
had seen in him a true revolutionary and allowed herself to
be carried off by what she supposed to be a romantic hero.
Learning of his treachery, she is completely unmoved by his
Andreevian theorizing and sees in him merely a contemptible
lackey:

> Masha: You would never have achieved the status
> of a Napoleon, but you might have achieved
> a cosy position and a good salary. (41)

Masha is an early example of a Lunacharskian heroine
whose emotions unerringly dictate to her the course to be
followed, while men vacillate, or allow treacherous oppor-
tunism to dictate their actions.

In *Another Sordid Tale* Lunacharsky parodies one of
Dostoevskii's humorous short stories - *A Sordid Tale* (1862)
(42). Here the superior official imposes himself on his
subordinate not, as in Dostoevskii's tale, at the latter's
wedding celebrations, but because he and his wife have had
their dacha raided by rioting peasants (a topical allusion).
In Dostoevskii's tale the element of farce derives from the
hopelessly embarrassing situation in which the incautious
bureaucrat places himself by allowing himself in a moment
of alcoholic bonhomie to invade the celebrations. Lunacharsky
makes very little of the actual situation, relying heavily
on a rather mechanically contrived series of farcical mis-
understandings: before leaving for work in the morning the
General's subordinate, Maletskii, receives a mysterious
anonymous note which (falsely) states that his wife is being
unfaithful to him. The General and his wife arrive unbeknownst
to Maletskii and are accommodated by his wife in the main bedroom. Maletskii deliberately returns unexpectedly during
the night, enters his dacha by way of the bedroom window, and
sets about the man he takes to be his wife's lover. The
General takes him for a rioting peasant, and pandemonium
ensues.

The Fugitive Political is more carefully structured
(43). The theme is the already familiar one of the identity
of vitality and emotional healthiness, of 'fullness of life',
with the revolutionary outlook. Into the family of a Constitutional Democrat there comes a fugitive political prisoner to
whom the Kadet, Turkhanov, reluctantly gives asylum. His

41. *Ibid.*, 22.

42. 'Eshche skvernyi anekdot', *ibid.*, 25-43.

43. 'Beglyi politik, *ibid.*, 45-65.

daughter Yuliya is an idealistic young woman who complains
to her father that instead of taking action they 'are
peacefully sitting, drinking tea with milk and cawing' (44).
Turkhanov is rapidly characterized as a long-winded but
politically inert 'idealist':

> We must let the long-suffering muzhik make a living
> ... that is our duty. Duty, my daughter, is a
> frightfully important thing ... Christ, and Kant
> ... and others besides all agreed ... you must do
> your duty or ... it's a bad do ... We'll have a
> right lot of anarchy, civilization will be de-
> stroyed, and we'll all be sent a-begging. (45)

The 'political' is in fact no 'political' at all, but
a criminal. He is soon exchanging significant looks with
Turkhanov's wife, who contrives to send her husband off to
town on an errand for a while. That night the criminal is
about to ransack the house, but is disturbed by the amorous
wife. The two of them are in turn disturbed by Yuliya. Her
mother gets away, but the criminal, who has given his name as
'Smith', finds himself confronted with a bright-eyed Yuliya
who urges him to let her join the Party and fight for the
people. 'Smith' is very much moved and confesses to her that
he is not worthy of her candour, but is a common burglar whose
real name is Mishka Merkulov. He leaves the house unburgled,
murmuring, 'It takes all kinds, it really does' (46). The
political stance of the characters straightforwardly reflects
their vitality or lack of it. The bumbling old cuckold is a
Kadet, 'Smith', the unprincipled but undoubtedly virile rogue,
declares himself to be a Maximalist (after his leader, Maksim),
while the uncorrupted human spirit instinctively sides with
the left-wing of the revolution.

The Bomb is another piece preoccupied with socio-
psychological questions (47). The old and new societies are
represented respectively by Prince Boris Ivanovich Kleshch-
Chernobyl'skii and Yurii, the housekeeper's 'nephew'. The
prince is a martinet who fines his servants for minor mis-
demeanours and lectures them on morality, even as he eyes
pornographic postcards, confiscated in St. Petersburg, which
to his indignation had been on sale 'at a generally accessible
price'. Against the ponderous hypocrisy of the prince is pitted
the simple perspicacity of Yurii who sets the prince in a rage.
The prince finds a bomb under his table, which is in fact merely

44. Ibid., 51.

45. Ibid., 50.

46. Ibid., 65.

47. 'Bomba', ibid., 67-86.

a toy which Yurii has made. He is panic-stricken, but is
'saved' by Yurii who does not know what all the fuss is about.
The prince then adopts him for having saved his life, and
justice is finally done (since it seems likely that Yurii is
in fact his illegitimate son by the housekeeper).

    The Slow Speed Society is yet another satire on liberal
politics (48). A meeting has been called to bring the leading
members of the local intelligentsia together in a united movement which will submit petitions and advice to the government.
Lunacharsky expresses his contempt for liberal intelligentsia
politics by having the characters expostulate on their visions
of the future Russia - visions which clearly can have no
political reality, and which have their foundation in the
psychological make-up of the characters themselves. The
'moderate Tolstoyan' Zhuchkov hopes 'to bring our intelligentsia
back to the old good-naturedness of the people, to cabbage
soup, buckwheat gruel, bathhouses ... even to cockroaches'.
He would 'give [the Jews] a scrap of land in Siberia and
let them run their own state', and would make Moscow once
more the capital of Russia [!] (49)

    This strange assortment of individuals, their social
position ranging from the wealthy local factory-owner to the
anarchistic revolutionary Gulyaev, is unable to agree on any-
thing, to the deep concern of the Chairman who is anxious to
see business completed so as to enable the meeting to adjourn
for dinner. Deadlock has been reached when they are invaded
by the local police who have been tipped off that a dangerous
conspiracy is under way, and everybody is arrested. Confronted with the brutally absurd might of the Law the 'politicians'
forget their phrases and fall in with the orders of the
gendarmerie. Only the daughter of a merchant's widow,
Verochka Melkina, is obstructive. She struggles to keep a
letter she has received from a left-wing youth, and protests
at the submissiveness of all the speechifiers, including even
Gulyaev.

    This is undoubtedly one of Lunacharsky's more effective
pieces. His gift for compromising the political standpoint of
his opponents by finding a suitably eccentric and ineffectual
mouthpiece, and his ability to exaggerate the tenets of each
ideology to the point of total absurdity produce here a
virtuoso performance. He again chooses an innocent young girl
as his positive heroine, the standard against which the other
characters are judged. This farce is one of the few of
Lunacharsky's works with a clearly autobiographical element.
In April 1900 Lunacharsky was arrested with all the participants

48. 'Obshchestvo maloi skorosti', *ibid.*, 87-122.

49. *Ibid.*, 102.

at a lecture he was giving to about a hundred members of the
Kiev intelligentsia on Ibsen. The police raided and General
Novitskii was summoned. He ordered the participants to separate
into groups of 'Jews, men and women'. Lunacharsky records that
some confusion resulted among those unsure whether to classify
themselves as Jews or women. The incident is repeated in the
farce where, in addition, the General 'discovers' Jews in the
teacher of German origin, Zeidel', and the Lutheran pastor,
Gimmel'ber (50).

A significant feature of Lunacharsky as a playwright emerges
from these farces. If the farcical situations are not always
well married to the farcical elements in the language, ideas or
personalities of the characters, they show the interpretation
which Lunacharsky gives to the dictum that ideas only mask
deeper interests. He shows in these farces the distortion of
ideals by self-interest, not only economic but primarily
psycho-sexual. An important corollary is that he sees the
ideals of pure youthful sexuality as having an almost selfless
and normative quality. The responsibility for the farcical
distortion of these ideals is laid by implication on the social
environment. Attention is, however, concentrated more immediately
on the psychologically based criticism of political ideals.

Lunacharsky did not neglect his talent for oratory during
the revolutionary period. Once again, as in the lecturing
campaign for Bolshevism in 1905, the philosophical tended to
drive out the political and he decided to devote a lecture
series to the history of religion. He lectured in various
further eduction institutions, but principally at the Polytechnic where he had no trouble in filling the main lecture
theatre. His topic, philosophical socialism, was of com-
pelling interest to the youthful truth-seeking public.
Various other leading lights of the time attended and debated
with him afterwards, including on a couple of occasions the
controversial preacher Grigorii Petrov who subsequently became
a member of the Second Duma (and was unfrocked and exiled upon
its dissolution). The proceeds from the lectures, which
Lunacharsky put at around 10,000 rubles, went to the Petrograd
Committee of the RSDRP (51).

A. Ya. Tairov, later director of the Moscow Kamernyi
Theatre, was to recall Lunacharsky's impact:

Through personal conversation, with his articles,
with his lectures in the Petersburg 'Circle of the

50. See Lunacharskii, 'V kievskoi Luk'yanovskoi tyur'me',
in *Vospominaniya i vpechatleniya*, 73-5.

51. *Velikii perevorot*, 42; *Vospominaniya i vpechatleniya*,
344, n. 78.

Young' which brought together all the young artists
of St. Petersburg, he sowed the seeds of Marx's
philosophy in our minds. In some the seeds germinated
quickly and in others they sprouted only many years
later.(52)

In such a forum, predominantly of young people, Aleksandr Deich
remembers, Lunacharsky read his modest new one-act play
Visitors in Solitary (53). Deich rightly comments that few
people remember the play (54). It is, in fact, a re-working of
Temptation, a re-presentation of the other play's underlying
idea in a guise adapted to the moment, and making use of
Lunacharsky's recent imprisonment with its attendant publicity.

The hero of *Visitors in Solitary*, a certain Gruzdev, is
in solitary confinement for marginal complicity in a political
offence: would it not be wisest to forget his principles and
live an obscure, comfortable life? This is the advice he
receives from a monstrous scaly hallucination which visits him.
He is not a political leader, but an artist; he merely agreed
to harbour a mysterious trunk for a radical friend who had
urged him to betray her to the police if it should be discovered. He is in prison on a political charge when his only
crime is to have been too honourable a man to betray this
Klarissa Lyudvigovna. His painting, his freedom, a beautiful
wife can all be his, whispers the monster, if he will only
recant. Gruzdev dismisses the monster and has a further
visitation, this time, suitably enough, from a Chernyshevskian
woman in white. She welcomes him to the ranks of martyrs for
the glorious future.

He who lived for himself is dead; like a shade
He sinks into the gulf of the past.
Heroes do not die.(55)

The temptations of Gruzdev and those of Manuel are almost
identical: in one case the scaly monster, in the other the
slimy Belial hold out matrimony and private life as an alternative to a life of active idealism. In this play a private
life is sacrificed on the altar of noble ideals, while Manuel
had hoped to gain strength from living a full, normal life to
sustain him in his preaching. The feeling of community is
made more pronounced here than in the earlier play: Gruzdev

52. 'Pamyati A.V. Lunacharskogo', *Vestnik Kommunisticheskoi
akademii*, L., No. 3, 1935, 33.

53. *Gosti v odinochke*, in *Idei v maskakh*, 205-21.

54. Aleksandr Deich, 'Dramaturgiya A.V. Lunacharskogo', in
Lunacharskii, *P'esy*, 7.

55. *Idei v maskakh*, 220.

is not aiming to change the world on his own; he is an honest and sensitive artist instinctively on the side of an existing revolutionary movement, and in his suffering he is one of a long succession of victims of the powers of darkness against which humanity must battle.

The action is contemporary and clearly set in Russia, whereas *Temptation* was set in Ravenna in the Middle Ages. The mode is no less fantastic and mythological, but where the mediaeval setting of *Temptation* harmonized with the mythological elements, in the contemporary setting of *Visitors in Solitary* the supernatural figures are not a little unexpected. No bridge is offered between the realism of the cell and the realistically treated non-realistic elements. There is nothing to indicate the non-real nature of the allegorical figures other than their extreme improbability in that setting. We are, of course, seeing with Gruzdev's eyes and he is delirious and dying, but this aspect is not skilfully handled. This very unease is splendidly exploited by Gerhart Hauptmann in his treatment of a child's delirium in *Hanneles Himmelfahrt* where the audience is itself unsure until the end of the play that the action is delirium, but where this final discovery makes it possible to view the preceding descent into fantasy in as 'scientific' a light as one could wish. Interestingly, here an artist is explicitly shown as being instinctively on the side of the revolutionaries (56).

1906 was a year of anti-climax. The conflict with the Mensheviks had begun to seem increasingly irrelevant in the light of the common tasks facing all members of the Social Democratic Party. According to Lunacharsky, the defeat of the Moscow uprising in December 1905 accelerated this realization. 'It was quite touching to watch Lenin and Martov, who were once such close friends and subsequently such implacable enemies, talking peacefully together and looking for points of contact'(57). As the government gained control of the country once again it was Lunacharsky who was chosen to chair many of the conciliatory sessions between the Party fractions (58). The Fourth Congress was held in Stockholm 10-25 April 1906 and Lunacharsky was to work out an agreement with the Mensheviks regarding reunification of the Central Committee of the Party.

> I have to say that the comrades took me for a ride
> in a rather unpleasant manner: I signed an agreement

56. There is a striking formal similarity between the apotheosis of Lunacharsky's *Tommaso Campanella* and the finale of *Gosti.*

57. *Velikii perevorot*, 36.

58. 'Bol'sheviki v 1905 godu', in Lunacharskii, *Siluety*, 476.

> with the Mensheviks to the effect that the new
> membership of the CC, a little over one third
> of which was to be composed of Bolsheviks nom-
> inated by us, would be ratified by the Congress
> unanimously. In the meantime, our faction,
> without warning me and apparently without any
> preliminary meeting, decided otherwise. As a
> result the whole Congress voted for the Bolsheviks,
> whose names came first on the list, while only the
> Menshevik majority voted for the Mensheviks, the
> Bolshevik delegates abstaining.(59)

This portent was significant. Reunification had little
chance of acceptance if, as Lunacharsky reports, Lenin saw
the question as being, 'Do we or do we not enter a reunited
Party controlled by the Mensheviks?' (60). At all events,
the split soon became irrevocable, with the Mensheviks
favouring adaptation to legal work within the new constitutional
framework and overall support for the Constitutional Democratic
Party, and the Bolsheviks moving, temporarily at least, towards
support for semi-terrorist 'partisan' groups. Lunacharsky's
relations with Plekhanov reached a new low point.

Another of Lunacharsky's hybrid works of fictionalised
political journalism appeared while the Congress had been in
full swing. 'An Interview with the Devil' satirizes the
proponents of compromise and gradual reform (61). Technically
it is an extremely able piece of journalism. Lunacharsky
first establishes his own system of values by choosing a
fantastic setting. The interviewer descends to meet the devil,
who, while he has something in common with the Ahriman Berdyaev
was accused of worshipping, is here much more specifically
represented as the un-revolutionary, sceptical, academic
politician who favours the path of negotiation and compromise.
He sits, not wholly dissimilar to Plekhanov, in his Voltairean
chair at his writing desk and smokes a cigar as he replies, at
first unwillingly, to the interviewer's promptings. His realm
is the realm of confusion and lethargy. His spouse is bore-
dom. Since Marx illuminated the political scene he has been
almost driven off it, since no one is now willing to believe
in the work of the devil. In response to more prompting from
his interviewer he concedes that he has a certain residual
influence: he has his puppets. These are the worldly-wise
but unenlightened actors in the Marxian comedy, sleep-walkers
whose actions are totally determined by the economic process.
They are like the victims of Fate in *Charudatta the Wise*
before they know the future.

59. *Velikii perevorot*, 39.

60. *Ibid.*, 38-9.

61. Anton Levyi[ps.], 'Interv'yu u cherta. Fel'eton', in
Vestnik zhizni, SPb., No. 3, 18 April 1906, 8, cols. 11-12.

'They must come to an understanding,' says the Devil,
'the top brass of the Civil Service and the top brass
of the Stock Exchange; the landowner must embrace the
merchant, and the professor enter in as the third
party in a union worthy of them [...]

My puppets will advance along the narrowest of
cornices, confidently putting their best professorial
foot forward. They are like sleep-walkers, drawn on
by the moon of the "great politics of the whole
people", great politics based on the principles of
"here's to you and here's to me", of "have your cake
and eat it too", of "more haste, less speed", and
other dogmas of the most scientific of ethics and
sociology.'

Behind the smokescreen the marriage of the
autocracy with the bourgeoisie will take place. The
issue will be a miserable little freedom delivered
by the official midwife, while the dangerous, blood-
stained, bright-eyed baby in another cot, which had
survived the onslaught of the Black Hundreds, will be
starved to death, to the babbling of oppositional
speeches from the Devil's learned puppets. *Pereat,
pereat libertas!* Long live the Party of the People's
Liberty'. (62)

Technically *An Interview with the Devil* is close to the
fantasias. It is an elaborate metaphor of Lunacharsky's
emotional response to liberalism and the Mensheviks' gradualism.
It demonstrates a link between his distaste for what he regards
as philosophical idealism and political liberalism. Each is
accused of the same faults - of succumbing to Ahriman, who for
Lunacharsky increasingly personifies a kind of *mauvaise foi*, a
negation of the revolutionary will.

When Lunacharsky characterized himself as 'a poet of the
Revolution' he pointed to the importance for him of the emotional
connotation of the Revolution (63). 'My whole outlook
militated against half-hearted positions, against compromise
and the masking of the bright maximalistic principles of true
revolutionary Marxism' (64). It is this emotional basis of his
beliefs which makes his ideas so amenable to figurative treatment.

62. *Ibid*.

63. *Velikii perevorot*, 31.

64. *Ibid*.

Lunacharsky tarried for a while in Finland on his way
home from the Congress. Here, as we have seen, he discussed
with Mikhailovskii the possibility of staging *The King's
Barber* in Riga. He and a number of other anti-Duma agitators
were arrested on a serious charge by the police, but acquitted
by a sympathetic Finnish court (65).

Lunacharsky supposes that the 'literary' prosecutions
which now began to mount up against him were connected with
rumours that he was a possible Bolshevik candidate for the
second Duma, for which elections were to be held in 1907 (66).
In May 1906 charges were brought against him in connection
with his article 'On the Character of the Present Moment'
(67). On 5 June the St. Petersburg Press Committee asked
the Court of Justice to bring charges against his edition of
Kautsky's 'The Russian and the American Worker' (68). On
23 December 1906 charges were brought against Lunacharsky
for his pamphlet against the Constitutional Democrats, *Three
Kadets*, the Press Committee accusing the author of 'incite-
ment to serious crime' (69). At this stage Lunacharsky called
in a solicitor and learned that he was liable to face a five-
or six-year term of imprisonment (70).

> The first years of revolution passed for me in
> feverish, exhausting and fragmented work which
> was not always effective. It not only exhausted
> me, but raised a whole series of doubts about
> Party organization and tactics [...]

> By February 1907 the situation had become insufferable.
> Severe overtiredness, the undermining of my health,
> extreme dissatisfaction with the course of events in
> the Party and the need to re-examine many things in

65. M.N. Lyadov, *Iz zhizni partii v 1903-1907 godakh.
Vospominaniya*, 172-6; *Literaturnoe nasledstvo*, 80, 740.

66. *Velikii perevorot*, 41.

67. Lunacharskii, 'K kharakteristike tekushchego momenta',
in *Nevskii sbornik*, vyp. 1, SPb., 1906, 1-20; Ermakov,
A. Lunacharskii, 29.

68. K. Kautskii, *Russkii i amerikanskii rabochii*, ed.
A. Lunacharskii, SPb., 1906, 89 pp.; V.N. Foinitskii,
'A.V. Lunacharskii i tsarskaya tsenzura', *Russkaya literatura*,
No. 4, 1975, 146.

69. Lunacharskii, *Tri kadeta. Pamflet*, SPb., 1907, 162 pp.;
Foinitskii, 'A.V. Lunacharskii', 145.

70. *Literaturnoe nasledstvo*, 80, 740.

> its past - all inclined me to emigration. A
> relative political calm provided the opportunity,
> and a number of threatened literary prosecutions
> provided an additional argument in favour of
> leaving.(71)

He set off for the Finland Station without his family and,
meeting no obstacles there, emigrated through Helsinki to
Hangö and thence, through Copenhagen, to Germany and Italy
(72). For Lunacharsky the first Russian Revolution was over.
He was thirty-one years old.

71. *Literaturnoe nasledstvo*, 82, 553.

72. *Velikii perevorot*, 43; *Literaturnoe nasledstvo*, 82, 740.

CONCLUSION

What, then, were the sources of Lunacharsky's erudite
'unseriousness', and of the revolutionary enthusiasm which
set him apart from other members of the intelligentsia?
What insights can we claim at the end of this 'socio-
psychological' study? From what we know of his childhood
we may surmise that his parents gave him more than merely
the usual intelligentsia preoccupations with radical politics and cultural self-improvement. His unconventional
family background can be seen to have given him a radical
drive which is wholly absent from such equally well-bred
contemporaries as Nikolai Berdyaev who came from secure and
conventional backgrounds. The importance of the time and
place of his schooling in Kiev in the 1890s has been evident.

There is a striking continuity from the literary
commentator and populariser of the schoolboy circles in Kiev
to the post-1917 Commissar of Enlightenment, without whose
introductory comments it sometimes seemed no theatre performance could commence, no work of classical or contemporary literature be published; from the fiery young debater of
Kiev and Vologda to the Bolshevik orator and agitator of
1917. From the outset Lunacharsky was accustomed to per-
forming before and winning the approval of an audience. His
erudition was a means to an end. Is it not here that we
find the explanation both of what Berdyaev saw as his
erudite superficiality, and of what Blok saw as his avoid-
ance of the worst failings of the intelligentsia (meaning,
perhaps, over-articulate political impotence?); a clue, at
least, to his post-revolutionary political longevity? There
is a continuity too from Lunacharsky's voluminous philosophical and polemical writings, heavy with emotive metaphor
and cosmic perspectives, to the political fantasy of his
stories and plays.

Lunacharsky himself was to recall in 1919 that, if Lenin approached Party matters as a practical politician of genius, his own approach in the early days was that of a philosopher, indeed of a poet of the revolution.

> For me it was a tragic but essential moment in the general evolution of the human spirit into the 'Pan-psyche'; it was the greatest, most definitive act in the process of 'god-building', the most dazzling and decisive step towards fulfilling the programme laid down by Nietzsche - 'The world is without meaning, but we must give it meaning'. (1)

This difference of approach was, amongst other things, to fuel the dispute between Lenin and Bogdanov, Lunacharsky, and the other 'Russian Machists' from 1908 onwards. The philosophy was much in evidence in his efforts to foster a proletarian culture in the decade before 1917.

If Lunacharsky had died in 1907 he would scarcely be remembered today. I hope, nevertheless, that the present study throws light on his later, more spectacular career.

---

1. *Velikii perevorot*, 31.

BIBLIOGRAPHY

L.=Leningrad, M.=Moscow, SPb.=St. Petersburg

Works by A.V. Lunacharskii

Lunacharskii used the following pseudonyms:

Antonov, 'Poslednie vybory'   Levyi, Anton, 'Interv'yu u Cherta'
Anyutin, Anatolii, 'Pokhorony'   Voinov, V., *Kak peterburgskie*
L-kii, 'Pershi kroki'

(a) Archival

'K portretu. Stikhotvorenie', MS, IMLI, f. 16, op. 1, ed. khr. 29, list 1.

'Kogda-b mogli vy zaglyanut' ... Stikhotvorenie', MS, IMLI, f. 16, op. 1, ed. khr. 28, listy 3-4.

Birth Certificate of A.V. Lunacharskii(copy), TsGALI, f.279, op. 2, ed. khr. 537.

'Mne snilos', chto ya stal tsvetkom ... Stikhotvorenie', MS, IMLI, f. 16, op. 1, ed. khr. 27.

'Muzyka. Difiramb bogu Dionisu. Poema', MS, 46 pp., IMLI, f. 16, op. 1, ed. khr. 30.

'Na grud' tvoyu solntse lobzan'e purpurnoe ... Stikhotvorenie', MS, IMLI, f. 16, op. 1, ed. khr. 28, listy 1-2.

Letter to Nik. Aleks. Popov, 1906, MS, TsGALI, f. 837, op. 1, ed. khr. 210.

'Tak stranno ... nezrimym ob"yat'em tomlen'e ... Stikhotvorenie',
MS, IMLI, f. 16, op. 1, ed. khr. 29, list 2.

'Zolotoe utro. Stikhotvorenie', MS, IMLI, f. 16, op. 1, ed.
khr. 26.

(b) Published

[Avenarius] *R. Avenarius. Kritika chistogo opyta. V populyarnom
izlozhenii A. Lunacharskogo. - Novaya teoriya pozitivnogo
idealizma (Holzapfel. Panideal). Kriticheskoe izlozhenie
A. Lunacharskogo*, M., 1905.

[Bogdanov] 'Aleksandr Aleksandrovich Bogdanov', *Pravda*, 85,
10 April 1928, 3.

'Bol'sheviki v 1905 godu', *Proletarskaya revolyutsiya*, 11
(46), 1925, 49-61.

'Dva liberala. (Ballada)'; *Proletarii*, Geneva, 16, 1905,
4.

'Elementy dushi', *Kur'er*, M., 29, 27 March 1903, 3.

Etyudy kriticheskie i polemicheskie, M., 1905.

'Filosof, kotoryi smeetsya', *Kur'er*, M., 27, 25 March 1903,
3.

'Idealist i pozitivist, kak psikhologicheskie tipy', *Pravda*,
1, 1904, 118-39.

Idei v maskakh, M., 1912.

'Interv'yu u Cherta. Fel'eton', *Vestnik zhizni*, SPb., 3,
18 April 1906, 3.

Iskushenie. Dramaticheskaya skazka v vol'nykh stikhakh,
M., 1922.

'Iz vologodskikh vospominanii', *Sever*, Vologda, 2, 1923,
1-5.

'Iz vospominanii o Zhane Zhorese', *Krasnaya niva*, 31,
28 July 1929, 12-13.

'K kharakteristike tekushchego momenta', *Nevskii sbornik*,
SPb., 1, 1906, 1-20.

'K yubileyu 9 yanvarya', *Proletarii*, Geneva, 13, 1905, 3-4.

Kak peterburgskie rabochie k tsaryu khodili, Geneva, 1905.
Published under the pseudonym V. Voinov.

Korolevskii bradobrei. P'esa v semi kartinakh, SPb., 1906.

Kryl'ya, M., 1905.

'Lenin iz krasnogo mramora. Otryvok iz neopublikovannoi stat'i', *Sovetskoe iskusstvo*, M.-L., 1, 2 January 1934, 1.

[Lunacharskii] *A.V. Lunacharskii. Neizdannye materialy, Literaturnoe nasledstvo*, 82, M., 1970.

[Lunacharskii] *A.V. Lunacharskii. Ukazatel' trudov, pisem, i literatury o zhizni i deyatel'nosti*, 2 vols., M., 1975-9.

'Malen'kie fantazii. Lunnyi svet, Skripach, Arfa', *Russkaya mysl'*, 11, 1902, 48-53.

'Marksizm i estetika. Dialog ob iskusstve', *Pravda*, M., 9-10, 1905, 391-419.

'Moris Meterlink', *Obrazovanie*, 10, 1902, 148-67; 11, 1902, 101-17.

'Mudryi Charudatta', *Pravda*, M., 9, 1904, 29-34.

'Neskol'ko vstrech s Georgiem Valentinovichem Plekhanovym', *Pod znamenem marksizma*, 5-6, 1922, 87-95.

'O khudozhnike voobshche i o nekotorykh khudozhnikakh v chastnosti', *Russkaya mysl'*, 2, 1903, 43-67.

'O natsionalizme voobshche i ukrainskom dvizhenii v chastnosti', *Ukrainskaya zhizn'*, M., 10, 1912, 9-22.

'Opyat' v Zheneve', *Komsomol'skaya pravda*, 284, 13 December 1927, 2-3.

'Osnovy pozitivnoi estetiki', *Ocherki realisticheskogo mirovozzreniya*, SPb., 1904, 113-82.

Ot Spinozy do Marksa. Ocherki po istorii filosofii kak mirosozertsaniya, M., 1925.

Otkliki zhizni, SPb., 1906.

'Pamyati Georgiya Valentinovicha Plekhanova', *Plamya*, Petersburg, 7, 16 June 1918, 2-4, [98-100].

'Pershi kroki sotsial-demokratichnogo rukhu v Kievi', *Ukrains'kii istorichnii zhurnal*, Kiev, 4, 1959, 121-32. Published under the pseudonym L-kii.

'Pesenka Aristida. Dlya srednego golosa', in B. Karagichev, *Romansy*, SPb., 1912.

110

P'esy, M., 1963.

'Pis'mo v redaktsiyu', *Izvestiya*, 14 January 1923, 5.

'Pokhorony', *Kur'er*, 27, 25 March 1903, 3. Published under the pseudonym Anatolii Anyutin.

'Poslednie vybory vo Frantsii', *Rabotnik*, Geneva, 5-6, May 1899, 278-89. Published under the pseudonym Antonov.

'Predislovie k dramolettam', *Teatr*, L., 2, 1966, 71-6.

'Printsessa Tyurandot', *Kur'er*, 27, 25 March 1903, 3.

Pyat' farsov dlya lyubitelei, SPb., 1907.

'Russkii Faust', *Voprosy filosofii i psikhologii*, 3, 1902, 783-95.

Siluety, M., 1965.

Sobranie sochinenii, 8 vols., M., 1963-7.

'Spinoza', *Kur'er*, 29, 27 March 1903, 3.

'Tragizm zhizni i belaya magiya', *Obrazovanie*, 9, section 2, 1902, 109-28.

Tri kadeta. Pamflet, SPb., 1907.

'Tsar v Parizhe', *Listok 'Rabotnika'*, Geneva, 2, December 1896, 13-16.

'V kievskoi Luk'yanovskoi tyur'me', *MOPR*, 5, October 1924, 26-7.

Velikii perevorot. (Oktyabr'skaya revolyutsiya), Pt. 1, Petersburg, 1919.

Vospominaniya i vpechatleniya, M., 1968.

Other works cited

Aksel'rod, P.B., 'Bor'ba zhelezno-dorozhnykh rabotnikov Shveitsarii s ikh ekspluatatorami', *Rabotnik*, Geneva, 3-4, 1897, 17-46.

Aksel'rod, P.B., *Istoricheskoe polozhenie i vzaimnoe otnoshenie liberal'noi i sotsialisticheskoi demokratii v Rossii*, Geneva, 1898.

Ashmarin, V., 'Korolevskii bradobrei', *Izvestiya VTsIK i Mossoveta*, 3, 4 January 1919, 4.

Bailes, Kendall E., 'Philosophy and Politics in Russian Social Democracy: Bogdanov, Lunacharsky and the Crisis of Bolshevism, 1908-1909'. Unpublished essay for the degree of Master of Arts in the Faculty of Political Science etc., Columbia University, New York, 1966.

Balashova, N., 'Bichuyushchii zhestokost' i zlobu', *Teatral'-naya zhizn'*, 16, 1968, 15.

Bel'tov, N., [i.e. G.V. Plekhanov], *K voprosu o razvitii monisticheskogo vzglyada na istoriyu*, SPb., 1895.

Berdyaev, N., 'Filosofskaya istina i intelligentskaya pravda', *Vekhi. Sbornik statei o russkoi intelligentsii*, 3rd ed., M., 1909.

Berdyaev, N., *Samopoznanie - opyt filosofskoi avtobiografii*, Paris, 1949.

Berdyaev, N., *Sub"ektivizm i individualizm v obshchestvennoi filosofii*, SPb., 1900.

Blok, Aleksandr, *Sobranie sochinenii*, 8 vols., M.-L., 1960-3.

Bogdanov, A.A., *Osnovnye elementy istoricheskogo vzglyada na prirodu*, SPb., 1899.

Bol'shaya sovetskaya entsiklopediya, 2nd ed., 51 vols., M., 1949-58.

Bolt, Robert, *State of Revolution*, London, 1967.

Bór., pseudonym [i.e. Józ. Konarski, alias J. Moszyński], [Kijów w czerwcu], *Przedświt*, London, 7, 1894, 28-9.

Bulgakov, Sergei, 'Ivan Karamazov (v romane Dostoevskogo "Brat'ya Karamazovy") kak filosofskii tip', *Voprosy filosofii i psikhologiii*, 1, 1902.

Chekhov, A.P., *Perepiska A.P. Chekhova i O.L. Knipper*, 3 vols., M., 1934.

Chukovskii, Kornei, *Sovremenniki*, M., 1962.

Chuprov, A.I., *Politicheskaya ekonomiya*, M., 1892.

Daniels, Robert V., *Red October. The Bolshevik Revolution of 1917*, London, 1967.

112

Danilov, S.S., *Ocherki po istorii russkogo dramaticheskogo teatra*, M.-L., 1948.

Deyateli revolyutsionnogo dvizheniya v Rossii, ed. Vl. Vilenskii-Sibiryakov *et al.*, 5 vols. (incomplete), 1927-34.

Dikshtein [Dickstein], S., *Kto chem zhivet*, Geneva, 1885.

Eidel'man, B., 'K istorii vozniknoveniya RSDRP', *Proletarskaya revolyutsiya*, 1, 1921, 20-67.

Eidel'man, B., 'Neskol'ko zamechanii po povodu vospominanii A.V. Lunacharskogo v knige *Velikii perevorot*', *Proletarskaya revolyutsiya*, 2(14), 1923, 615-17.

Entsiklopedicheskii slovar' T-va 'Br. A. i I. Granat i K^o', 7th ed., 58 vols., M., [1910]-48.

Ermakov, A., *A. Lunacharskii*, M., 1975.

Ermolaev, I.E., 'Moi vospominaniya', *Sever*, Vologda, 3-4, 1923, 1-28.

Fedorchenko, L.[S.], 'Pervye shagi sotsial-demokratii v Kieve', *Katorga i ssylka*, XXVII, 1926, 21-33.

Fitzpatrick, Sheila, *The Commissariat of Enlightenment: Soviet Organization of Education and the Arts under Lunacharsky*, Cambridge, 1970.

Fitzpatrick, Sheila, *Education and Social Mobility in the Soviet Union, 1921-1934*, Cambridge, 1979.

Foinitskii, V.N., 'A.V. Lunacharskii i tsarskaya tsenzura', *Russkaya literatura*, 4, 1975, 145-7.

Gnesina, E., 'Vospominaniya o Lunacharskom', *Sovetskaya muzyka*, 3, 1967, 70-2.

[Gor'kii] *M. Gor'kii. Neizdannaya perepiska, Arkhiv A.M. Gor'kogo*, XIV, M., 1976.

Ivanyukov, I., *Padenie krepostnogo prava v Rossii*, SPb., 1882.

Karvatskii, A. Ya., 'Iz deyatel'nosti pervykh rabochikh kruzhkov v Kieve', in *Put' revolyutsii. Sbornik pervyi. Sotsial-demokraticheskoe dvizhenie v Kieve (90-e gody)*, Kiev, Izd. Kievskogo gubkoma K.P.(b)U., 1923, 92-101. See also Krovatskii, A.Ya.

Kautsky, K., *Russkii i amerikanskii rabochii*, SPb., 1906.

Kennan, George, *Siberia and the Exile System*, 2 vols., New York, 1891.

Khomenko, V., *Anatolii Vasil'evich Lunachars'kii*, Kiev, 1974.

Kindersley, Richard, *The First Russian Revisionists: a Study of Legal Marxism in Russia*, Oxford, 1962.

Kokhno, I.P., *Cherty portreta*, Minsk, 1972.

Kokhno, I.P., 'Dorevolyutsionnaya dramaturgiya A.V. Lunacharskogo', *Uchenye zapiski Karel'skogo pedagogicheskogo instituta*, 18, 1967, 25-37.

Kokhno, I.P., 'Poslednyaya ssylka Lunacharskogo', *Sever*, Petrozavodsk, 11, 1971, 124-8.

Kokhno, I.P., 'Vologodskaya ssylka Lunacharskogo', *Literaturnoe nasledstvo*, 82, M., 1970, 603-20.

Konarski, Józ., see Bór., and Moshinskii.

Kr[anikhfel'd], Vl., ['Korolevskii bradobrei'] , *Mir bozhii*, 6, section II, 1906, 63-4.

Krovatskii, A.Ya., 'Moi vospominaniya', *K dvadtsatipyatiletiyu pervogo s"ezda Partii (1898-1923)*, M.-Pb., 1923. See also Karvatskii, A.Ya.

Krupskaya, N., 'Pamyati Anatoliya Vasil'evicha Lunacharskogo', *Vestnik Kommunisticheskoi akademii*, 1, 1934, 81-5.

Krupskaya, N., *Vospominaniya*, M.-L., 1926,

Kursinskii, A., ['Korolevskii bradobrei'], *Vesy*, 9, 1906, 69-70.

[Lenin] *V.I. Lenin i A.V. Lunacharskii. Perepiska, doklady, dokumenty, Literaturnoe nasledstvo*, 80, M., 1971.

Lepeshinskii, P.N., *Na povorote*, 2nd ed., L., 1925.

Lesevich, V.V., *Chtoe takoe nauchnaya filosofiya?*, SPb., 1891.

Lunacharskaya, I.A., 'K nauchnoi biografii A.V. Lunacharskogo', *Russkaya literatura*, 4, 1979, 110-27.

Lunacharskaya-Rozenel', N.A., *Pamyat' serdtsa. Vospominaniya*, 3rd rev. ed., M., 1975.

Lyadov, M.N., *Istoriya Rossiiskoi Sotsialdemokraticheskoi Rabochei Partii*, 2 vols., SPb., 1906.

114

Lyadov, M.N., *Iz zhizni partii v 1903-7 godakh. Vospominaniya*, M., 1956.

Manilov, V., 'K istorii vozniknoveniya sotsial-demokraticheskogo dvizheniya v Kieve (80-e - 90-e gody)', *Put' revolyutsii. Sbornik pervyi. Sotsial-demokraticheskoe dvizhenie v Kieve (90-e gody)*, Kiev, Izd. Kievskogo gubkoma K.P.(b)U., 1923, 18-79.

Martow, L., pseudonym, *Geschichte der russischen Sozialdemokratie*, Berlin, 1926.

Men'shchikov, L. [P.], *Okhrana i revolyutsiya*, 2 parts, M., 1925-32.

Minskii, N., 'Istoriya moego redaktorstva', in his *Na obshchestvennye temy*, SPb., 1909, 193-9.

Mirski, D.S., 'A Russian Letter', *London Mercury*, 1920, December, 207-9; 1921, February, 427-9; April, 657-9; August, 414-18.

Monyukov, V., 'Pokazyvali Sevastopol'tsy', *Sovetskaya kul'tura*, M., 19, 14 February 1961, 3.

Moshinskii, I. (Józef Moszyński) [pseudonym, i.e. Józef Konarski], *Na putyakh k 1-mu s"ezdu R.S.-D.R.P. 90-tye gody v kievskom podpol'e*, M., 1928. See also Bór.

Nemirovich-Danchenko, Vl. Iv., 'Lyudi teatra ne zabudut Lunacharskogo', *Literaturnaya gazeta*, 29 December 1933.

Ocherki istorii Moskovskoi organizatsii KPSS, 1883-1965, M., 1966.

Nevskii, V., *Ocherki po istorii Rossiiskoi Kommunisticheskoi partii*, 2nd ed., 1, L., [1926].

'Pamyati A.V. Lunacharskogo', *Vestnik Kommunisticheskoi akademii*, 3, 1935, 23-39.

Panchenko, N., 'Avtografy A.V. Lunacharskogo v Pushkinskom dome', *Russkaya literatura*, 2, 1966, 212-16.

Perazich, V., *Yu.D. Mel'nikov. (Na zare sotsial-demokraticheskogo dvizheniya Ukrainy)*, Khar'kov, 1930.

Piyashev, N., '"Arestovannyi" Ibsen. Stranichka iz biografii A.V. Lunacharskogo', *Teatr*, 2, 1966, 77-8.

Plavnik, A., 'Pervye shagi budushchego narkoma', *Neman*, Minsk, 8, 1968, 177-80.

Plekhanov, G.V., *Filosofsko-literaturnoe nasledie G.V. Plekhanova*, 3 vols., M., 1973-4.

Plekhanov, G.V., *Perepiska G.V. Plekhanova i P.B. Aksel'roda*, 2 vols., M., 1925.

Plekhanov, G.V., *Sochineniya*, 20 vols., M., 1923-7.

Plekhanov, G.V., see also Bel'tov, N.

Reisner, M.A., *Russkii absolyutizm i evropeiskaya reaktsiya*, SPb., 1906.

Shapiro, L.B., *The Communist Party of the Soviet Union*, 2nd rev. ed., London, 1970.

Semenovskii, O., 'A.V. Lunacharskii i ukrainskaya literatura', *Sovetskaya Ukraina*, 12, 1958, 164-7.

Shul'gin, V., *Pamyatnye vstrechi*, M., 1958.

Sonkin, A.[M.] , 'Vospominaniya', in *K dvadtsatipyatiletiyu pervogo s"ezda Partii. (1898-1923)*, M.-Pb., 1923, 64-8.

Stepnyak[-Kravchinskii] , S.[M.] , *Podpol'naya Rossiya*, London, 1893.

Struve, P.B., *Kriticheskie zametki k voprosu ob ekonomicheskom razvitii Rossii*, SPb., 1894.

Tait, A.L., 'Lunacharskii's Russian *Faust*', *Germano-Slavica*, III, 3, Spring 1980, 189-203.

Tarutin, An., 'K istorii revolyutsionnogo dvizheniya i politicheskoi ssylki v Vologde. (Po povodu "Vospominanii" A.V. Lunacharskogo i I.E. Ermolaeva)', *Sever*, Vologda, 2, 1924.

Thun, Alphons, *Geschichte der revolutionären Bewegungen in Russland*, Leipzig, 1883.

Trifonov, N.A., 'Lunacharskii v gorode Lenina', *Zvezda*, 11, 1965, 183-7.

Trifonov, N.A., 'O Lunacharskom-poete', *Russkaya literatura*, 4, 1975, 137-44.

Trifonov, N.A. and Shostak, I.F., 'A.V. Lunacharskii i "Moskovskoe delo" 1899 goda', *Literaturnoe nasledstvo*, 82, M., 1970, 587-602.

Tuchapskii, P.L., *Iz perezhitogo. Devyanostye gody*, Odessa, 1923.

Tugan-Baranovskii, M.I., *Promyshlennye krizisy v sovremennoi Anglii*, SPb., 1894.

Turovskaya, M., *Ol'ga Leonardovna Knipper-Chekhova*, M., 1959.

Valentinov, Nikolai, [i.e. Nikolai Vladislavovich Vol'skii], *Encounters with Lenin*, London, 1968.

Vladimirskii, M., 'Iz istorii sotsial-demokraticheskoi organizatsii. (Lichnye vospominaniya)', in *Pervyi s"ezd RSDRP. Mart 1898 goda. Dokumenty i materialy*, M., 1958, 162-5.

Vodovozov, V.V., 'V.D. Novitskii. (Iz lichnykh vospominanii)', in General V.D. Novitskii, *Iz vospominanii zhandarma*, L., 1929, 1-12.

Vyadro, Sh., 'Dobryi drug Ukrainy', *Raduga*, Kiev, 3, 1974, 136-42.

Yaroshevskii, I.P., 'Put' A.V. Lunacharskogo k nauchnomu ateizmu v dorevolyutsionnyi period', *Trudy Tadzhikskogo politekhnicheskogo instituta*, vyp. 6, *Uchenye zapiski kafedry obshchestvennykh nauk*, 1971, 222-38.